Workbook

SOCIAL STUDIES

GROWTH OF A NATION

PEARSON

Scott
Foresman

Editorial Offices: Glenview, Illinois • Parsippany, New Jersey • New York, New York
Sales Offices: Parsippany, New Jersey • Duluth, Georgia • Glenview, Illinois
Coppell, Texas • Ontario, California • Mesa, Arizona

www.sfsocialstudies.com

Program Authors

Dr. Candy Dawson Boyd
Professor, School of Education
Director of Reading Programs
St. Mary's College
Moraga, California

Dr. Geneva Gay
Professor of Education
University of Washington
Seattle, Washington

Rita Geiger
Director of Social Studies and
    Foreign Languages
Norman Public Schools
Norman, Oklahoma

Dr. James B. Kracht
Associate Dean for
    Undergraduate Programs
    and Teacher Education
College of Education
Texas A & M University
College Station, Texas

Dr. Valerie Ooka Pang
Professor of Teacher Education
San Diego State University
San Diego, California

Dr. C. Frederick Risinger
Director, Professional
    Development and Social
    Studies Education
Indiana University
Bloomington, Indiana

Sara Miranda Sanchez
Elementary and Early
    Childhood Curriculum
    Coordinator
Albuquerque Public Schools
Albuquerque, New Mexico

Contributing Authors

Dr. Carol Berkin
Professor of History
Baruch College and the
    Graduate Center
The City University of New York
New York, New York

Lee A. Chase
Staff Development Specialist
Chesterfield County
    Public Schools
Chesterfield County, Virginia

Dr. Jim Cummins
Professor of Curriculum
Ontario Institute for Studies
    in Education
University of Toronto
Toronto, Canada

Dr. Allen D. Glenn
Professor and Dean Emeritus
College of Education
Curriculum and Instruction
University of Washington
Seattle, Washington

Dr. Carole L. Hahn
Professor, Educational Studies
Emory University
Atlanta, Georgia

Dr. M. Gail Hickey
Professor of Education
Indiana University-Purdue
    University
Ft. Wayne, Indiana

Dr. Bonnie Meszaros
Associate Director
Center for Economic Education
    and Entrepreneurship
University of Delaware
Newark, Delaware

ISBN 0-328-08180-9

21 VON4 14 13

Contents

Summarize

Directions: Read the passage below. Then fill in the circle next to the correct answer.

In 1607, English colonists established a new settlement at Jamestown. From the start, the colony faced a number of serious problems. The settlement's water supply was of poor quality and caused many to become sick. The nearby swamps were swarming with disease-carrying mosquitoes. Food was in short supply. And conflicts with neighboring Native American groups sometimes turned violent.

In spite of these problems, the Jamestown colonists managed to survive. The introduction of tobacco farming helped put the colony on solid ground economically. The marriage of a colonist to a chief's daughter helped bring peace—for a while. Many new colonists arrived. These factors helped make Jamestown survive—and become the first permanent English colony in North America.

1. Which sentence best summarizes paragraph 1?

    Ⓐ Jamestown's water supply was almost its undoing.

    Ⓑ The colonists failed to build a friendship with Native Americans.

    Ⓒ Jamestown faced a series of problems in its early years that threatened its survival.

    Ⓓ Mosquitoes were not considered to be dangerous.

2. Which of the following is NOT one of the main ideas in paragraph 1?

    Ⓐ Jamestown was founded in 1607.

    Ⓑ Jamestown faced a shortage of food.

    Ⓒ The colony was located near a mosquito-infested swamp.

    Ⓓ Colonists grew tobacco.

3. Which sentence best summarizes paragraph 2?

    Ⓐ Jamestown overcame its problems and survived to become the first permanent English colony in North America.

    Ⓑ The marriage of a colonist to a Native American helped Jamestown.

    Ⓒ Native Americans loved the colonists' tobacco.

    Ⓓ Jamestown was founded in 1607.

4. Which of these is NOT an important detail in paragraph 2?

    Ⓐ Colonists in Jamestown raised tobacco.

    Ⓑ Jamestown did not have enough food.

    Ⓒ Marriage between a colonist and a chief's daughter helped stop fighting for a while.

    Ⓓ New colonists arrived in Jamestown to help strengthen the colony.

Notes for Home: Your child learned to summarize, or tell the main idea, of a passage.
Home Activity: Read a newspaper story with your child. Together, summarize the main idea and look for supporting details.

Vocabulary Preview

Directions: Match each vocabulary word to its meaning. Write the number of the word on the blank next to its meaning

1. Ice Age	_13_ Trade network shaped like a triangle
2. glaciers	_12_ Large farms with many workers
3. migrate	_7_ The movement of people, animals, plants, and ways of life between Europe and the Americas
4. agriculture	_9_ The first law-making assembly in an English colony
5. culture	_3_ To move
6. colony	_4_ A system for producing and distributing goods and services
7. Columbian Exchange	_6_ A settlement far from the country that rules it
8. cash crop	_2_ Thick sheets of ice
9. House of Burgesses	_14_ Conflict between the British and French and Native American allies
10. natural resource	_8_ A crop grown for profit
✓**11.** economy	_1_ A long period of time during which Earth's climate was colder than it is today
12. plantations	_5_ The way of life of a group of people
13. triangular trade route	_10_ A material found in nature that people can use, such as trees or water
14. French and Indian War	_11_ The knowledge of how to grow crops and raise farm animals

Directions: Choose the word from the box below that best completes each sentence. Write the word on the line provided.

Stamp Act	checks and balances	Industrial Revolution
Declaration of Independence	Bill of Rights	manifest destiny
republic	Cabinet	abolitionist
constitution	political party	

1. The idea of _____ was the belief that the United States should expand west to the Pacific Ocean.

2. A _____ is a system in which people elect representatives to make laws and run the government.

3. A system to keep branches of government from gaining too much power is a

   system of _____.

4. A person who called for an end to slavery everywhere was

   known as an _____.

5. The President's advisors were part of the _____.

6. The _____ was added to the Constitution to guarantee certain freedoms.

7. The _____ placed a tax on printed goods used by the colonists.

8. A written plan of government is a _____.

9. The _____ was a change in the way goods were produced.

10. The _____ explained why the colonies believed they must declare independence from Britain.

11. An organized group of people who share a common view of what government

    should do is a _____.

Notes for Home: Your child has learned the vocabulary words from the Overview.
Home Activity: Have your child create flash cards for each vocabulary word and its definition. Use the cards to quiz your child on meanings and spellings.

Lesson 1: Connections Across Continents

Directions: Complete the outline with information from this lesson. You may use your textbook.

Humans in North America up to 1492

I. The First Americans

   A. The first people in North America may have crossed a _____ _____ from Asia.

   B. The first people got their food by _____.

   C. About 7,000 years ago, people began to practice _____.

II. Native American Cultures

   A. Groups living in the same region of North America developed similar _____.

   B. Groups relied on available resources.

      1. Eastern Woodland people hunted in forests.

      2. On the Great Plains, people hunted _____.

      3. In the Southwest, people relied on agriculture.

      4. In the Northwest, coastal waters and _____ supplied plentiful food.

III. Cultures Mix

   A. Inventions promote trade and travel.

   B. Europeans arrived in _____ in 1492.

   C. The _____ changed life in the Eastern and Western Hemispheres.

 Notes for Home: Your child has learned about the early history of human beings in North America.
Home Activity: Help your child develop an illustrated time line of the time period of 20,000 years ago to 1492.

Name _____ Date _____

Lesson 2: Life in the Colonies

Directions: Answer the following questions on the lines provided. You may use your textbook.

1. What attracted so many people from Europe to come to North America in the 1600s? What was the name and location of the first permanent English colony in North America?

_____

_____

2. What factor led to the foundation of colonies in the New England area?

_____

_____

3. What were the names and major economic features of the three regions of England's colonies?

_____

_____

_____

_____

_____

4. Under what circumstances did most Africans come to North America?

_____

_____

5. Describe the conflict that lead to the French and Indian War. What was the effect of this war?

_____

_____

_____

_____

_____

Notes for Home: Your child learned about the growth and development of the earliest European colonies in North America.
Home Activity: Ask your child to summarize the causes and effects of European colonization.

Compare Maps at Different Scales

Directions: Study the map below and answer the questions.

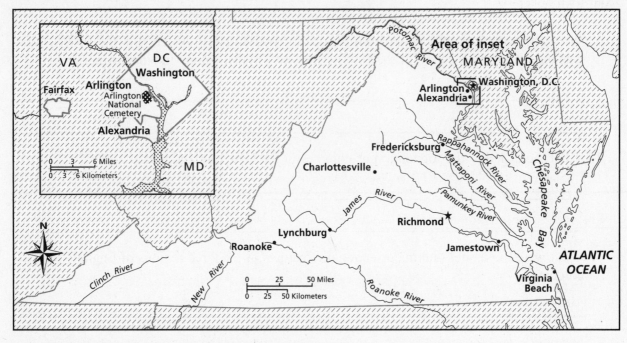

1. Describe the small scale map pictured above.

_____

_____

2. Describe the large scale map pictured above.

_____

3. Which map would you use to locate attractions in Washington, D.C.?

_____

4. Which map would help you to find the distance between cities in Virginia?

_____

5. Why are both small-scale and large scale maps useful?

_____

_____

_____

 Notes for Home: Your child learned to measure distances on a map using a scale and to tell the difference between large-scale maps and small-scale maps.
Home Activity: Practice finding the scale on maps that you see in newspapers and other materials.

Lesson 3: Revolution and Constitution

Directions: Using information from this lesson, circle the term in parentheses that best completes each sentence.

1. When news of the Stamp Act reached the 13 Colonies, many colonists reacted with (joy, anger).

2. Colonists who opposed British rule came to be known as (Patriots, Loyalists).

3. In 1775, colonists prepared to (fight, elect) their British rulers.

4. During the Revolutionary War, George Washington served as (general, president).

5. In the early battles of the war, George Washington led the army to several (defeats, victories).

6. A turning point in the Revolutionary War was when the French came to the aid of the (British, Patriots).

7. The new government for the independent colonies was to be a (republic, monarchy).

8. In 1787, delegates met in Philadelphia to create a (constitution, Declaration of Independence).

9. Some people in the United States worried that the Constitution gave the government too (little, much) power.

10. Fears about individual liberties were calmed by the addition of a Bill of (Rights, Independence).

Notes for Home: Your child learned about the Revolutionary Era in the United States.
Home Activity: Have your child recount the tale of how the United States first grew apart from Great Britain, then fought for its independence, then established a new government.

© Scott Foresman / Growth of a Nation

Lesson 4: A Growing Nation

Directions: Suppose you were going to write an article about the first years of the United States. Use the chart below to help you get started. You may use your textbook.

The First Years of the United States	
WHO was the first President?	
WHAT problem existed in his Cabinet?	
HOW did President Jefferson help the United States grow?	
WHAT was the Industrial Revolution?	
WHAT was "manifest destiny"?	
WHO were the abolitionists?	

Notes for Home: Your child learned a brief overview of the first half-century of United States history.
Home Activity: Use library or online sources to look up more about the items presented in the Fact File on page 33.

© Scott Foresman / Growth of a Nation

Name _____ Date _____

Use Parallel Time Lines

Directions: Use the time lines below to answer the following questions.

MARTINA

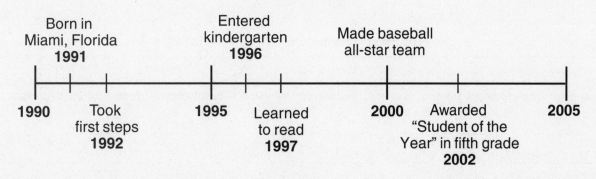

Born in
Miami, Florida
1991

Entered
kindergarten
1996

Made baseball
all-star team

1990

Took
first steps
1992

1995

Learned
to read
1997

2000

Awarded
"Student of the
Year" in fifth grade
2002

2005

TONY

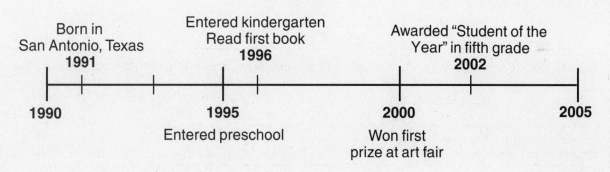

Born in
San Antonio, Texas
1991

Entered kindergarten
Read first book
1996

Awarded "Student of the
Year" in fifth grade
2002

1990

1995

Entered preschool

2000

Won first
prize at art fair

2005

1. In what ways have Tony and Martina had similar lives?

   _____

   _____

2. In what ways have Tony and Martina had different educations?

   _____

3. What can you learn about Tony and Martina based on the events of 2000?

   _____

   _____

4. What can you learn about Tony and Martina based on the events of 2002?

   _____

Notes for Home: Your child learned to read parallel time lines.
Home Activity: With your child, make parallel time lines of your day. Compare and contrast events.

Vocabulary Review

Directions: Use the vocabulary words from the Overview to complete each item.
Use the numbered letters to answer the clue that follows.

1. A change in the way goods were produced

   — — <u>—</u> — — — — — — — —
        1

   — — — — — — — — — —

2. The movement of people, animals, plants, and ways of life between Europe and the Americas

   — — — — — — <u>—</u> — — — — — — — — —
         14

3. An early British tax on printed goods

   — — <u>—</u> — — — — —
     5

4. Thick sheets of ice

   — — — — — <u>—</u> — —
        19

5. A system in which people elect representatives to make laws and run the government

   — — — — — — <u>—</u> —
        9

6. A system to keep branches of government from gaining too much power

   — — — — — — — — — — — — — — — — <u>—</u> —
               25

7. An organized group of people who share a common view of what government should do

   — — — <u>—</u> — — — — — — — — —
      4

8. A long period of cold temperatures

   — — — — — <u>—</u>
        17

9. A person who called for the end of slavery everywhere in the United States

   — — — — — — — — <u>—</u> — — —
          23

10. The belief that the United States should expand west to the Pacific Ocean

    — — — — — — — <u>—</u> — — — — — —
           21

11. To move

    — — — — <u>—</u> —
       7

12. A system for producing and distributing goods and services

    — — — <u>—</u>
      20

13. A material found in nature that people can use

    — — — — — — — — — <u>—</u> — —
           6

Workbook

14. The way of life of a group of people

— — — — — — —
$\overline{}$ $\overline{}$ $\overline{}$ $\overline{}$ $\underset{22}{\overline{}}$

15. The knowledge of how to grow crops and raise farm animals

— — — — — — — — —
$\underset{24}{}$

16. A written plan of government

— — — — — — — — — —
$\underset{3}{}$

17. Large farms with many workers

— — — — — — — — — —
$\underset{10}{}$

18. A President's advisors

— — — — — —
$\underset{2}{}$

19. Conflict between the British and French and Native American allies

— — — — — — — — — — — — — — —
$\underset{13}{}$

20. Crop grown for profit

— — — — — — — —
$\underset{18}{}$

21. Added to the Constitution to guarantee certain freedoms

— — — — — — — — — —
$\underset{8}{}$

22. A settlement located far away from the country that rules it

— — — — — —
$\underset{11}{}$

23. The first law-making assembly in an English colony

— — — — — — — — — — — — —
$\underset{12}{}$

24. Trade networks shaped like triangles

— — — — — — — — — — —
$\underset{15}{}$ $\underset{16}{}$

— — — — —

Clue: created by Thomas Jefferson

$\overline{1}$ $\overline{2}$ $\overline{3}$ $\overline{4}$ $\overline{5}$ $\overline{6}$ $\overline{7}$ $\overline{8}$ $\overline{9}$ $\overline{10}$ $\overline{11}$ $\overline{12}$ $\overline{13}$

$\overline{14}$ $\overline{15}$ $\overline{16}$ $\overline{17}$ $\overline{18}$ $\overline{19}$ $\overline{20}$ $\overline{21}$ $\overline{22}$ $\overline{23}$ $\overline{24}$ $\overline{25}$

Notes for Home: Your child learned the vocabulary from the Overview unit.
Home Activity: Talk to your child about how the vocabulary words relate to what they learned in the unit about American history.

Name _____ Date _____

Overview Project This Just In

Report breaking news in American history. In a group, choose an important event that you have learned about in American history. Then report the event in a press conference.

1. The event that we chose is _____ .

2. My role in the press conference is (✔) one

    ____ news reporter   ____ expert

    ____ government official   ____ other: _____

3. Here are some details about the event:

    What happened: _____

    Where and when the event took place: _____

    Who was involved: _____

    Effects or importance of the event: _____

4. Here are some questions and answers that we will ask and answer in our news conference:

    News Reporter: _____

    Expert: _____

    News Reporter: _____

    Other _____ : _____

✔ Checklist for Students

____ We chose an event in America's history.

____ We found information about the event.

____ We answered questions about the event.

____ We made a poster about the event to use in our press conference.

____ We presented our press conference to the class.

 Notes for Home: Your child learned how to report important details of an event in a press conference.
Home Activity: Watch a news program with your child. Discuss what important facts are reported about each event, and why the events might be important to the region where the events occurred.

Main Idea and Details

Directions: Fill in the circle next to the correct answer.

> Many people believe slavery in the United States ended with the Emancipation Proclamation. This idea is not completely accurate. The Emancipation Proclamation did outlaw slavery, but slavery continued in some areas.
>
> Only certain people were declared free by the Emancipation Proclamation. Those people were slaves who lived in Confederate states that were fighting against the Union. Slaves who lived in border states that were fighting for the Union were not granted freedom by the proclamation. Also unaffected were those slaves living in Southern areas already under Union control.
>
> Although the Emancipation Proclamation granted legal freedom to slaves living in Confederate states that were fighting against the Union, those states did not recognize Lincoln's laws. Therefore, the slaves saw no change.
>
> All slavery in the United States officially ended in December of 1865 with the passage of the Thirteenth Amendment to the Constitution.

1. How did the Emancipation Proclamation affect slavery?
   - Ⓐ It freed all slaves in all states.
   - Ⓑ It freed slaves in Union territory.
   - Ⓒ It freed slaves in some states, but not in others.
   - Ⓓ It did not free slaves.

2. Which slaves were NOT declared free by the Emancipation Proclamation?
   - Ⓐ slaves who wanted to fight for the Union
   - Ⓑ only African American women and children
   - Ⓒ those in border states and areas under Union control
   - Ⓓ only male slaves in border states

3. Why did slavery continue in Confederate states fighting against the Union?
   - Ⓐ Those states did not recognize Lincoln's laws.
   - Ⓑ The Union allowed it.
   - Ⓒ The Thirteenth Amendment had not been passed.
   - Ⓓ Those slaves did not want to move to the North.

4. What officially ended all slavery in the United States?
   - Ⓐ the Emancipation Proclamation
   - Ⓑ the passage of the Thirteenth Amendment to the Constitution
   - Ⓒ the Civil War
   - Ⓓ the Confederate states

Notes for Home: Your child learned about identifying the main idea and details of a passage.
Home Activity: With your child, choose a magazine or newspaper article of interest and work together to identify the article's main idea and details.

Vocabulary Preview

Directions: Match each vocabulary word to its meaning. Write the vocabulary
word on the line provided. Not all words will be used. You may use your glossary.

sectionalism	states' rights	secede
slave codes	Missouri Compromise	Confederacy
Underground Railroad	Fugitive Slave Law	Union
free state	Compromise of 1850	border state
slave state	Kansas-Nebraska Act	civil war

1. _____ to break away from

2. _____ state located between the Union and the Confederacy

3. _____ plan in which California entered the United States as a
free state and the Fugitive Slave Law was passed

4. _____ states that remained loyal to the United States government

5. _____ state in which slavery was not allowed

6. _____ law which stated that escaped slaves had to be returned
to their owners, even if they had reached Northern states
where slavery was not allowed

7. _____ law allowing the people of Kansas and Nebraska to
decide whether they would allow slavery in their territory

8. _____ organized, secret system set up to help enslaved people
escape from the South to freedom in the North or Canada

9. _____ loyalty to a section or part of the country rather than to
the whole country

10. _____ laws to control the behavior of slaves

11. _____ government formed by the seven seceding states, also
known as the Confederate States of America

12. _____ state in which slavery was legally allowed

© Scott Foresman / Growth of a Nation

Notes for Home: Your child learned the vocabulary terms for Chapter 1.
Home Activity: Help your child learn the vocabulary terms by having him or her form comparisons
between pairs of terms, such as *free state* and *slave state*, *Union* and *Confederacy*, and so on.

Lesson 1: North and South Grow Apart

Directions: Complete the compare-and-contrast table using information from
Lesson 1. You may use your textbook.

Topic	In the North	In the South	Similar or Different?
The way of life in 1850		Slavery was allowed in Southrn St	
Point of view on tariffs on imported goods			
Point of view on the buying and selling of manufactured goods			
Point of view on slavery			

Notes for Home: Your child learned about the different views of the North and the South during the mid-1800s.
Home Activity: With your child, discuss instances when your child's opinion or point of view might differ from that of a friend. Brainstorm positive ways to resolve or live with these differences.

Recognize Point of View

Point of view is the way a person looks at or thinks about a topic or situation and describes it. A person's point of view may be affected by his or her experiences and way of life.

Directions: Read the following poem. It was written by a Southern woman during the time when the South had to produce its own goods because it was blockaded by the North. Answer the questions that follow.

> My homespun dress is plain, I know;
>   My hat's palmetto, too.
> But then it shows what Southern girls
>   For Southern rights will do.
> We send the bravest of our land
>   To battle with the foe,
> And we will lend a helping hand
>   We love the South, you know.
> Hurrah! Hurrah!
>   For the sunny South so dear.
> Three cheers for the homespun dress
>   That Southern ladies wear.

1. What is the topic of the poem?

   _____

2. What words does the writer use to show how she feels about Southern soldiers?

   _____

3. What words does the writer use to show how she feels about the South?

   _____

4. How do you think the writer feels about supporting the South in the war? How do you know?

   _____

   _____

   _____

   _____

   _____

Notes for Home: Your child learned to identify the writer's point of view.
Home Activity: With your child, discuss a family situation or a situation at school in which two people had different points of view. Help your child recognize that different points of view can come from different goals or experiences.

© Scott Foresman / Growth of a Nation

Name _____ Date _____

Lesson 2: Resisting Slavery

Directions: Categorize each term in the box by writing it in the column of the correct category below. You may use your textbook.

performed acts of cruelty	pretended to be sick
broke the tools they used	separated family members
learned to read	enforced slave codes
required permission to leave plantation	formed the Underground Railroad
used physical punishment	worked slowly

Methods of Controlling Slaves	Ways Slaves Resisted

Directions: Write the missing cause or effect on the line provided. You may use your textbook.

1. **Cause:** Slaves suffered cruel, harsh treatment.

   Effect: _____

2. **Cause:** _____

   Effect: Slave owners tried to prevent slaves from gathering and meeting with one another.

3. **Cause:** Captive Africans aboard the Spanish vessel *Amistad* seized the ship and ended up in the United States.

   Effect: _____

   _____

Notes for Home: Your child learned how slaves reacted to the treatment they received.
Home Activity: With your child, discuss how he or she feels when treated unfairly. Relate this feeling to how the slaves reacted when they were treated harshly and unfairly.

Lesson 3: The Struggle Over Slavery

Directions: Match each item in the first column to its clue or description in the second column. Write the number of the item on the line before its description.

1. Missouri Compromise

2. Fugitive Slave Law

3. Compromise of 1850

4. Kansas-Nebraska Act

5. *Uncle Tom's Cabin*

6. Dred Scott decision

7. John Brown's plan

8. Abraham Lincoln

9. Stephen Douglas

____The Supreme Court ruled that slaves were not citizens of the United States and had no rights.

____ This book described the cruelties of slavery and won over many people to the abolitionist cause.

____ The people of each territory were allowed to decide whether it should be free or slave.

____ "If slavery is not wrong, then nothing is wrong. . . . [But I] would not do anything to bring about a war between the free and slave states."

____ Escaped slaves had to be returned to their owners, even if they had reached Northern states where slavery was not allowed.

____ A plan to attack pro-slavery people with weapons from the arsenal at Harpers Ferry further divided the North and the South in 1859.

____ The number of slave states and free states was kept balanced when Missouri was allowed into the Union as a slave state and Maine as a free state.

____ "Each state . . . has a right to do as it pleases on . . . slavery."

____ California became a free state, and the Fugitive Slave Law was passed.

© Scott Foresman / Growth of a Nation

Notes for Home: Your child learned about struggles over slavery that threatened to tear the United States apart.
Home Activity: With your child, choose a current controversial issue from the newspaper. Discuss citizens' opposing views and the divisions that can develop.

Lesson 4: The First Shots Are Fired

Directions: Sequence the events in the order in which they occurred by numbering them from 1 to 8. You may use your textbook.

_____ Lincoln asks Union states for troops to put down the Confederate rebellion.

_____ Abraham Lincoln is elected President of the United States.

_____ Some states are angered by Lincoln's call for troops. Virginia, Arkansas, Tennessee, and North Carolina secede and join the Confederacy.

_____ The Confederate States of America, or the Confederacy, is formed.

_____ The Confederates attack Fort Sumter, which is surrendered two days later. The Civil War has started.

_____ Jefferson Davis, president of the Confederacy, asks for the surrender of Union-held Fort Sumter in Charleston, South Carolina.

_____ The Southern states of South Carolina, Alabama, Florida, Mississippi, Georgia, Louisiana, and Texas secede.

_____ By Lincoln's inauguration on March 4, 1861, the Confederacy has control of most of the forts and military property in the South.

Directions: Explain each of the following points of view from the time of the American Civil War. You may use your textbook.

1. Explain the goal Lincoln and his supporters hoped to achieve by fighting the Civil War.

   _____

   _____

2. Explain the goal Southerners hoped to achieve by fighting the Civil War.

   _____

   _____

3. Why do you think Northerners called Southerners "rebels"?

   _____

   _____

   _____

Notes for Home: Your child learned how to determine the sequence of events for the beginning of the Civil War.
Home Activity: With your child, look over a previous lesson. Ask your child to tell the sequence of events in that lesson.

Vocabulary Review

Directions: Choose the vocabulary word from the box that best completes each sentence. Write the word on the line provided. Not all words will be used.

sectionalism	states' rights	secede
slave codes	Missouri Compromise	Confederacy
Underground Railroad	Fugitive Slave Law	Union
free state	Compromise of 1850	border state
slave state	Kansas-Nebraska Act	civil war

1. The _____ was made up of states that remained loyal to the United States government.

2. The _____ allowed California to be admitted to the Union as a free state.

3. _____ is the idea that people of a state can choose the laws that best fit their needs.

4. South Carolina was the first state to _____ from the Union.

5. The _____ preserved the balance between free and slave states.

6. The states that seceded from the Union formed the _____.

7. The _____ allowed people in certain areas to determine whether or not their territory would allow slavery.

8. Although some former slaves had reached the North and found freedom, the

_____ said they had to be returned to their owners.

9. _____ did not allow slaves to own land.

10. Slavery was illegal in California and any other _____.

11. Harriet Tubman became famous for helping slaves escape to freedom on the

_____.

Notes for Home: Your child learned the vocabulary terms for Chapter 1.
Home Activity: Have your child practice using the vocabulary terms in sentences of his or her own.

Workbook

Vocabulary Preview

Directions: Circle the vocabulary term that best completes each sentence.

1. The (Anaconda Plan, Reconstruction) was a three-part war strategy to crush the South during the Civil War.

2. Slavery was abolished by the (Thirteenth Amendment, Fourteenth Amendment) to the Constitution.

3. The (First Battle of Bull Run, Battle of Gettysburg) lasted three days and was one of the most important battles of the Civil War.

4. African Americans became U.S. citizens under the (Fourteenth Amendment, Thirteenth Amendment) to the Constitution.

5. At the (Battle of Antietam, Battle of Vicksburg), Union forces blockaded the city and bombarded it for 48 days.

6. (Segregation, Sharecropping) is the separation of blacks and whites.

7. Both the North and the South instituted the (blockade, draft) to get men to fight in the war.

8. The (Gettysburg Address, Emancipation Proclamation) granted freedom to slaves in any Confederate states that were still battling the Union.

9. The time after the war when the country was rebuilding and healing is known as (Reconstruction, segregation).

10. The (black codes, blockade) kept supplies from reaching Southern soldiers.

11. One of the early battles of the war was the (Battle of Gettysburg, First Battle of Bull Run).

12. People in many U.S. cities paid their respects to President Lincoln after his (assassination, impeachment).

13. The (Freedmen's Bureau, Emancipation Proclamation) was established to help former slaves after the war.

14. All male citizens received the right to vote with the ratification of the (Thirteenth Amendment, Fifteenth Amendment) to the Constitution.

15. The (Emancipation Proclamation, Jim Crow laws) enforced separation of blacks and whites.

16. Republicans in Congress called for the (total war, impeachment) of President Andrew Johnson.

Notes for Home: Your child learned the vocabulary terms for Chapter 2.
Home Activity: With your child, review each vocabulary term and its definition to make sure the term fits in the sentence. Then make your own sentences using the vocabulary terms.

Lesson 1: The Early Stages of the War

Directions: Complete each compare-and-contrast table with information about the Union and the Confederacy. You may use your textbook.

	Supporters of the North	Supporters of the South
Reason for fighting		

	Northerners	Southerners
Believed advantage over the opposition		

	Union	Confederacy
War strategies		

Notes for Home: Your child learned about different attitudes toward war and different strategies used by the North and South during the Civil War.
Home Activity: With your child, discuss possible problems the Union and the Confederacy might have had to consider when forming their war strategies. Ask your child what could have gone wrong in each case.

Lesson 2: Life During the War

Directions: For each main idea, write a supporting detail on the line provided. You may use your textbook.

1. **Main Idea:** News of the war spread in many ways.

   Detail: _____

   _____

2. **Main Idea:** As the war continued, both sides had trouble getting more soldiers.

   Detail: _____

   _____

   _____

3. **Main Idea:** Most of the soldiers who died in the Civil War did not die in battle.

   Detail: _____

   _____

4. **Main Idea:** The Civil War did not begin as a war against slavery.

   Detail: _____

   _____

5. **Main Idea:** African Americans who wished to serve in the war were not treated the same as white soldiers.

   Detail: _____

   _____

6. **Main Idea:** Women contributed to the war effort in many ways.

   Detail: _____

   _____

   _____

Notes for Home: Your child learned to identify the main idea and supporting details of a reading selection.
Home Activity: With your child, look over a previous lesson. Ask your child to point out the main ideas and then identify supporting facts and details.

Lesson 3: How the North Won

Directions: Match each term in the box with its clue. Write the term on the line provided.

Battle of Gettysburg	Ulysses S. Grant	total war
Gettysburg Address	Battle of Vicksburg	Robert E. Lee
Anaconda Plan	William Tecumseh Sherman	Appomattox Court House

1. Place where Generals Lee and Grant met to discuss the terms of the Confederates' surrender of the Civil War _____

2. "I would rather die a thousand deaths." _____

3. President Lincoln made a short speech at a ceremony to dedicate a national cemetery. In his speech, Lincoln inspired the Union to keep fighting for a united nation and the end of slavery. _____

4. A method of warfare designed to destroy the opposing army and the people's will to fight
_____

5. This three-day battle began on July 1, 1863. It was one of the most important battles of the Civil War. It was an important victory for the North and a costly battle for both sides.
_____

6. Head of the Union forces in the Battle of Vicksburg _____

7. The surrender of this battle by the Southerners cut the Confederacy in two.
_____

8. The Union blockade at the Battle of Vicksburg was part of this strategy to gain control of the Mississippi River and weaken the Confederacy. _____

9. Led soldiers in a destructive "March to the Sea" _____

Notes for Home: Your child learned how the North used strategies to win the Civil War.
Home Activity: With your child, brainstorm strategies for winning a game such as checkers, chess, or cards. Discuss the advantages of using a strategy to defeat an opponent.

Read a Road Map

A road map shows roads, cities, and places of interest. Drivers use road maps to figure out how to get from one place to another.

Directions: Use the road map to answer the following questions.

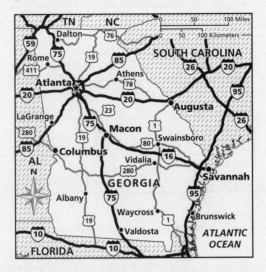

1. General Sherman's army probably walked and rode horses from Atlanta to Savannah, Georgia. What major roads might you take today to drive between these two cities?

   _____ 75, 16 _____

2. What major city would you pass through when traveling along this route from Atlanta to Savannah? _____ Macon _____

3. According to this map, what other roads might you take to travel from Atlanta to Savannah? _____ 75, 16 _____

4. Examine the map. Why do you think General Sherman's march was known as the "March to the Sea"? _____ because ~~they got~~ they got to the
   Sea _____

   _____

5. General Sherman's army left Savannah and went to South Carolina. If you were to drive from Savannah to South Carolina today, what major road might you take?

   _____ 95 _____

Notes for Home: Your child learned how to read a road map.
Home Activity: With your child, look at a road map of your state. Together, determine the most direct route from your city to one of your state's borders. Next, find the most scenic route.

Lesson 4: The End of Slavery

Directions: Define each term or phrase. Use a separate sheet of paper if you need more room. You may use your textbook.

1. Reconstruction _____

   _____

2. Thirteenth Amendment _____

   _____

3. black codes _____

   _____

   _____

   _____

4. Freedmen's Bureau _____

   _____

5. Ku Klux Klan _____

   _____

6. Fourteenth Amendment _____

   _____

7. Jim Crow laws _____

   _____

8. sharecropping _____

   _____

   _____

Notes for Home: Your child learned about how the United States changed after the Civil War.
Home Activity: With your child, review the series of changes that took place during Reconstruction and discuss who benefited from each change.

© Scott Foresman / Growth of a Nation

Vocabulary Review

Directions: Use the vocabulary words from Chapter 15 to complete the following sentences. Write the correct word in the space provided. You may use your textbook.

1. _____ is the separation of blacks and whites.

2. The shutting off of an area by troops or ships to keep people and supplies from moving in

   or out is known as a _____.

3. At the Battle of _____, Union forces blockaded the city and bombarded it with cannon fire by land and sea for 48 days.

4. _____ is the practice of renting land from a landowner and paying rent with a portion of the crop produced on that land.

5. The murdering of a government or political leader is known as an _____.

6. Laws that denied blacks the right to vote or take part in jury trials were known as

   _____.

7. A method of warfare that destroys not only the opposing army but also the people's will to

   fight is known as _____.

8. In the Battle of _____, Union and Confederate forces clashed near the town of Sharpsburg in Maryland.

9. The First Battle of _____, one of the early battles of the Civil War, was won by the Confederates.

10. The _____ was established to help the more than 4 million former slaves after the war.

11. _____ refers to the rebuilding of the country after the Civil War.

12. The Battle of _____ lasted three days and was one of the most important battles of the Civil War.

13. _____ laws enforced the separation of blacks and whites.

14. The _____ Plan was a war strategy designed to "squeeze" the Confederacy.

Notes for Home: Your child learned the vocabulary terms for Chapter 2.
Home Activity: With your child, analyze the relationships among the vocabulary terms for this unit. Begin by having your child place each term on a time line for the Civil War era.

© Scott Foresman / Growth of a Nation

Name _____ Date _____

Use with Page 118.

UNIT 1 Project   We Interrupt This Program

Directions: In a group, present a special report about an event described in this unit. Group members should choose a role and complete the assignment for that role.

1. The event that we chose is _____

2. My role in the news program is (✔)

   ____ news anchor   ____ reporter   ____ government official   ____ citizen

3. News Anchor: Write a summary of the event.

   _____

   _____

4. Reporter: Write questions to ask the government official and the citizen.

   _____

   _____

5. Government Official: Describe the event from your point of view.

   _____

   _____

6. Citizen: If you are an eyewitness, write a description of what you saw. If you were involved in the event, tell what happened from your point of view.

   _____

   _____

✔ **Checklist for Students**

_____ We chose an event.

_____ We chose a role to play in the news program.

_____ We wrote about the event from the point of view of our assigned role.

_____ Our group made a banner and background for our news program.

Notes for Home: Your child learned how to report important details of an event in a news program.
Home Activity: Watch a news program with your child. Discuss what important facts are reported about each event, and why each event might be important.

Workbook

Sequence

Directions: Sequence means the order in which events take place. Dates, times of
day, and clue words such as *first, next, then, after, finally, during,* and *meanwhile*
help signal the order of events. Use page 125 of your textbook to answer the
following questions. Fill in the circle next to the correct answer.

1. Which of the following occurred before construction began on the National Road?
   - Ⓐ The steamboat was invented.
   - Ⓑ People began using automobiles.
   - Ⓒ The country's first railroad was built.
   - Ⓓ The telegraph was invented.

2. According to the essay, what happened at the same time that the nation's transportation systems were advancing?
   - Ⓐ People were relying on stagecoaches.
   - Ⓑ Communications were also improving.
   - Ⓒ The National Road was nearing completion.
   - Ⓓ Radio was invented.

3. Which of the following occurred first?
   - Ⓐ The Pony Express started delivering mail.
   - Ⓑ "Horseless carriages" began appearing on roads.
   - Ⓒ The country's first railroad was built.
   - Ⓓ The transcontinental railroad was completed.

4. Which words tell you that the telegraph was developed after the start of the Pony Express?
   - Ⓐ "started delivering mail"
   - Ⓑ "in the following year"
   - Ⓒ "at the same time"
   - Ⓓ "even the Pony Express seemed slow"

5. Based on the essay, which happened last?
   - Ⓐ Samuel Morse developed a way of sending telegraph messages.
   - Ⓑ The telephone was invented.
   - Ⓒ A transcontinental telegraph was completed.
   - Ⓓ Radio communication was invented.

Notes for Home: Your child learned to sequence events and to understand the relationship between
events in a sequence
Home Activity: Provide your child with a list of events from his or her life in random order. Have your child
list them in the proper sequence.

Vocabulary Preview

Directions: Write each vocabulary word from Chapter 3 beside its example or description. You may use your textbook.

1. _____ area of land set aside for Native Americans

2. _____ African American pioneer

3. _____ business that delivered mail from Missouri to California in just ten days

4. _____ law that offered free land to American citizens and immigrants who were willing to start new farms on the Great Plains

5. _____ period when thousands of people went to search for gold

6. _____ use of new ideas to make tools that improve people's lives

7. _____ Great Plains farmer

8. _____ invention that sent messages along wires using electricity

9. _____ person who starts a new business hoping to make a profit

10. _____ battle in which Crazy Horse helped lead the Lakota to victory against United States forces

11. _____ when cowboys guided huge herds of cattle north to new railroad lines extending across the Great Plains

12. _____ settler who claimed land through the Homestead Act

13. _____ new settler

14. _____ railroad across the continent

Notes for Home: Your child learned the vocabulary terms for Chapter 3.
Home Activity: Encourage your child to tell or write a story using at least five of these words.

Lesson 1: Rails Across the Nation

Directions: Write the number of each item in Column A on the blank next to its description in Column B.

Column A	Column B
1. stagecoach	_____ told Union Pacific workers that they were scaring away the buffalo
2. Pony Express	_____ place where the Union Pacific and the Central Pacific met
3. telegraph	_____ horse-drawn wagons that traveled in regular stages
4. Samuel Morse	_____ invention that sent messages along wires using electricity
5. Union Pacific	_____ developed a way to send telegraph messages
6. Central Pacific	_____ part of transcontinental railroad that ran east from Sacramento, California
7. Red Cloud	_____ part of transcontinental railroad that ran west from Omaha, Nebraska
8. General William Tecumseh Sherman	_____ major natural obstacle to the Central Pacific
9. Promontory Point, Utah Territory	_____ business that delivered mail from Missouri to California in just ten days
10. Sierra Nevada	_____ warned Native American leaders that they could not stop the locomotive

Notes for Home: Your child learned about the building of the first transcontinental railroad.
Home Activity: Talk to your child about travel between the East and West today. How do people usually make this journey, and how long does it take?

Read a Time Zone Map

Directions: A time zone is a region in which all places have the same time. Time zone maps show different time zones. Study the map below and answer the questions that follow.

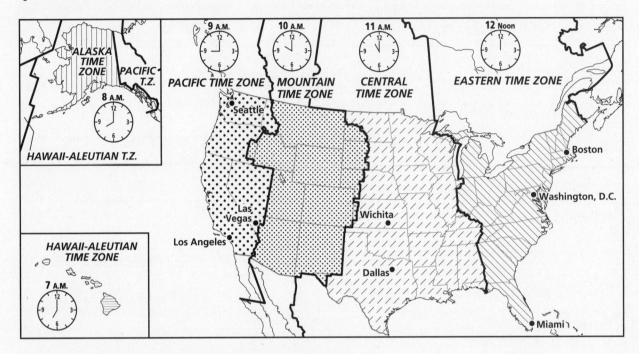

1. How many times zones exist in the United States?

   _____

2. Does the time become earlier or later as you move from east to west across the United States?

   _____

3. In what time zone is Miami located?

   _____

4. If it is 11 A.M. in Seattle, what time is it in Dallas?

   _____

5. Suppose you want to call a friend when he gets out of class at 1 P.M. in Hawaii. At what time should you make your call from Washington, D. C.?

   _____

Notes for Home: Your child learned to read a time zone map.
Home Activity: Help your child use the Internet or library resources to locate a world time zone map. Together, use the map to calculate differences between your time zone and time zones in other parts of the world.

Directions: Suppose that you are an American moving west on the Oregon Trail during the mid-1800s. Write a diary entry about your travels. Describe the people you meet and the challenges and opportunities you face along the way.

_____

_____

_____

_____

_____

_____

_____

_____

_____

_____

_____

_____

_____

_____

_____

_____

_____

_____

_____

_____

_____

_____

_____

© Scott Foresman / Growth of a Nation

Notes for Home: Your child learned about the westward expansion of the United States.
Home Activity: Study the map and time line on pages 136–137 with your child. Discuss what it might have been like to live in the changing United States during each period.

Lesson 2: Pioneers on the Plains

Directions: Using information from the lesson, circle the term in parentheses that best completes each sentence.

1. The government hoped that the (Homestead Act, sodbusters) would encourage pioneers to move to the Great Plains.

2. The famous novel *O Pioneers!,* by (Benjamin Singleton, Willa Cather), describes homesteaders' changing feelings about the Great Plains.

3. Europeans' desire to move to the Great Plains was so strong it became known as ("America Fever," the "Great American Desert").

4. African American pioneers called themselves (homesteaders, exodusters), after a book in the Bible that tells the story of Moses leading the Israelites out of slavery.

5. (Grasshoppers, Technology) helped make life easier for Great Plains farmers.

Directions: In the space below, write a letter to a friend as a pioneer on the Great Plains in the 1860s. Describe the hardships and the opportunities you face.

Dear _____ ,

_____

_____

_____

_____

_____

_____

Your Friend,

_____

© Scott Foresman / Growth of a Nation

Notes for Home: Your child learned about the settlement of the Great Plains during the late 1800s and how new technologies helped these settlers.
Home Activity: Review the Fact File on page 143 with your child. Then talk with your child about technologies that have helped improve your daily lives.

Read Climographs

Directions: A climograph shows the temperature and the average precipitation of a place. Look at the climograph below. Then answer the questions that follow.

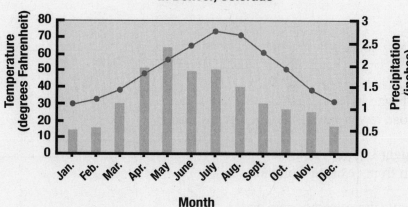

Average Temperature and Precipitation in Denver, Colorado

KEY
Line graph shows temperature.
Bar graph shows precipitation.

1. Which month received the greatest precipitation in Denver?

_____

2. What generalization can you make about the relationship between precipitation and temperature in Denver?

_____

_____

3. What is the warmest season in Denver?

_____

_____

4. What is the driest season in Denver?

_____

_____

5. How would you summarize the climate of Denver overall?

_____

Notes for Home: Your child learned to read a climograph.
Home Activity: Work with your child to compare and contrast the climate where you live with the climate in Denver, Colorado.

© Scott Foresman / Growth of a Nation

Lesson 3: Cowboys and Miners

Directions: Complete the outline with information from this lesson. You may use your textbook.

Life in the West

I. Cattle Drives

   A. Cattle drives were a way for ranchers to get their cattle to _____ in the East.

      1. The drives began in _____ and ended in Great Plains railroad towns such as Dodge City, Kansas.

      a. The Goodnight-Loving Trail, established by _____ in 1866, ran from Texas to Colorado.

   B. By the late 1880s, cattle drives came to an end.

      1. _____ began fencing in their lands with barbed wire to keep cattle off their farmland.

      2. Once _____ reached Texas, it was no longer necessary for ranchers to drive their cattle north.

II. Dreams of Gold

   A. During the California _____, thousands of people moved west in search of gold.

      1. By 1850, California had enough people to become a _____.

   B. When _____ discovered gold in the Rocky Mountains, miners began searching for gold all over the West.

      1. The flood of newcomers created opportunities for _____ like Luzena Stanley Wilson and Levi Strauss.

   C. The mining boom had lasting effects in the West.

      1. San Francisco, California, and _____ are two examples of important cities that emerged from supply stations for miners.

Notes for Home: Your child learned about the events that changed the American West.
Home Activity: Discuss with your child what it might have been like for you and your family to move west in search of gold during the mid-1800s.

© Scott Foresman / Growth of a Nation

Lesson 4: War in the West

Directions: Answer the following questions on the lines provided. You may use your textbook.

1. What changes took place in the West during the late 1800s that threatened the Native American way of life?

   _____

   _____

   _____

   _____

2. Why did the United States government try to move Native Americans to reservations?

   _____

   _____

3. Why was the Battle of Little Bighorn both a victory and a defeat for Native Americans?

   _____

   _____

   _____

   _____

4. Why did Chief Joseph agree to surrender?

   _____

   _____

5. What happened at Wounded Knee in 1890 and what was its significance?

   _____

   _____

   _____

Notes for Home: Your child learned how western expansion of the United States affected Native American groups.
Home Activity: Help your child use Internet or library sources to find information about Native American groups that once lived in your region.

Vocabulary Review

Directions: Use each of the vocabulary terms from Chapter 3 in a sentence. Write the sentences on the lines provided. You may use more than one term in a sentence. You may use your glossary.

Pony Express	homesteader	gold rush
telegraph	sodbuster	entrepreneur
transcontinental railroad	exoduster	reservation
pioneer	technology	Battle of Little Bighorn
Homestead Act	cattle drive	

_____

_____

_____

_____

_____

_____

_____

_____

_____

_____

_____

_____

_____

_____

_____

 Notes for Home: Your child learned the vocabulary terms for Chapter 3.
Home Activity: Create flashcards of these terms and their meanings to quiz your child.

Vocabulary Preview

Directions: Match each vocabulary word to its meaning. Write the number of the word on the blank next to its meaning.

1. investor

2. corporation

3. stock

4. monopoly

5. free enterprise

6. consumer

7. human resource

8. capital resource

9. prejudice

10. diversity

11. sweat shop

12. labor union

13. strike

_____ tool or machine that a company can use to produce goods and services

_____ share of a company

_____ variety

_____ when workers refuse to work to try to force business owners to meet their demands

_____ people who work to produce goods and services

_____ business that is owned by investors

_____ person who buys or uses goods and services

_____ system in which people are free to start their own businesses and own their own property

_____ group of workers who join together to fight for improved working conditions and better wages

_____ unfair negative opinion about a group of people

_____ hot, cramped workshop

_____ person who gives money to a business or project hoping to gain a profit

_____ company that has control of an entire industry

Notes for Home: Your child learned the vocabulary terms for Chapter 4.
Home Activity: Help your child use media sources to find current examples of the use of these terms.

Lesson 1: Inventors Change the World

Directions: Complete the chart with details from this lesson. You may use your textbook.

Inventor	Invention	Significance
		Changed the way people communicated
Thomas Edison		
	Method for making carbon filaments	
	Electric Streetcar	
Orville and Wilbur Wright		

Notes for Home: Your child learned about inventions that changed the United States at the turn of the twentieth century.
Home Activity: Ask your child whether and how these inventions affect your daily lives today.

Write an Outline

Directions: An outline is a written plan for organizing information about a subject. Look at the outline below. Then answer the questions that follow.

Andrew Carnegie

I. Childhood

   A. Born in Scotland

   B. Moved to the United States as a boy

II. Young adulthood

   A. Worked to help support his family rather than attending school

   B. Read on his own and attended night classes

III. Adulthood

   A. Business career

      1. Worked his way up in jobs at telegraph and railroad companies

      2. Made large amounts of money by making shrewd investments

      3. Became rich by building a huge steel empire

   B. Supporter of charitable causes

      1. Gave away millions of his fortune

      2. Is especially well known for supporting libraries

1. What is the main topic of this outline?

_____

2. How is the biographical information in this outline organized?

_____

3. What evidence supports the idea that education was important to Carnegie?

_____

4. According to the outline, how did Carnegie become wealthy?

_____

5. According to the outline, what were two main aspects of Carnegie's adult life?

_____

_____

Notes for Home: Your child learned to organize and read information in an outline.
Home Activity: Help your child outline the main ideas of a magazine or newspaper article.

Lesson 2: The Rise of Big Business

Directions: Using information from this lesson, circle the term in parentheses that best completes each sentence.

1. A new process for making (steel, iron) helped spark a boom in industry in the late 1800s.

2. Carnegie built his fortune by (buying, selling) a number of businesses involved in the steel-making process.

3. (Railroad, Oil) companies became the nation's first large corporations.

4. Corporations are owned by (investors, employees).

5. By selling (stock, capital resources), corporations can raise money to help their businesses grow.

6. Standard Oil became a (free enterprise, monopoly) by gaining control of the nation's oil industry.

7. The oil industry boomed in the early 1900s along with the rise of the (automobile, electric) industry.

8. In a free enterprise system, (business owners, consumers) decide what to produce and what to charge for products and services.

9. A company's employees are its (human resources, capital resources).

10. The rise of big business in the late 1800s helped the United States become the world's leading producer of (manufactured goods, natural resources).

Notes for Home: Your child learned about the rise of big business in the late 1800s and early 1900s.
Home Activity: Use a newspaper to read with your child about some of the issues facing big businesses today.

© Scott Foresman / Growth of a Nation

Lesson 3: New Americans

Directions: Fill in the blanks with information from this lesson. You may use your textbook.

Between 1880 and 1920, more than _____ immigrants arrived in the United States. Before 1890, most came from countries in _____. After that time, most came from _____. Many came to escape poverty, hunger and a lack of jobs. Some, such as Russian Jews, came in search of _____.

Millions of immigrants arriving on the East Coast passed through _____. Here they were checked for illnesses and asked questions about their plans. Chinese immigrants stopped at _____. The purpose of this stop was to ensure that they had _____ already living here. Many were forced to remain there for weeks or even longer. Once allowed into the United States, most immigrants had to find a _____ and a place to live. Many had to learn a new _____, and some faced the hardship of _____.

Directions: Suppose you are an immigrant arriving on Ellis Island in the late 1800s. Write a diary entry describing your experience. You may use a separate sheet of paper if you need more space.

_____

_____

_____

_____

_____

_____

_____

_____

Notes for Home: Your child learned about the era of immigration between 1880 and 1920.
Home Activity: Help your child use library or Internet resources to learn more about the immigrant experience in America at the turn of the century.

Lesson 4: The Labor Movement

Directions: Complete the chart with information from this lesson. You may use your textbook.

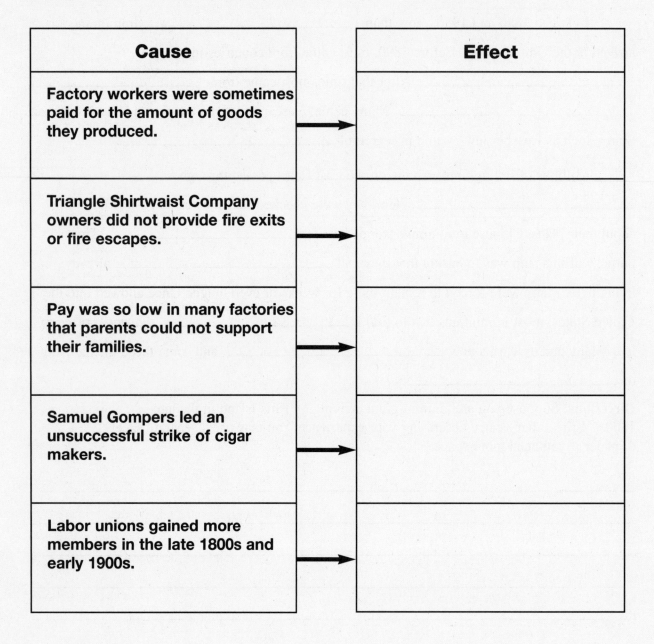

Cause	Effect
Factory workers were sometimes paid for the amount of goods they produced.	
Triangle Shirtwaist Company owners did not provide fire exits or fire escapes.	
Pay was so low in many factories that parents could not support their families.	
Samuel Gompers led an unsuccessful strike of cigar makers.	
Labor unions gained more members in the late 1800s and early 1900s.	

Notes for Home: Your child learned about the early days of the labor movement.
Home Activity: Discuss with your child how the labor movement of the late 1800s and early 1900s still affects workers today. Talk about current labor laws, labor unions, and strikes. Refer to events in the news and/or the jobs of people your child knows.

© Scott Foresman / Growth of a Nation

Vocabulary Review

Directions: Use the vocabulary terms from Chapter 4 to complete the crossword puzzle.

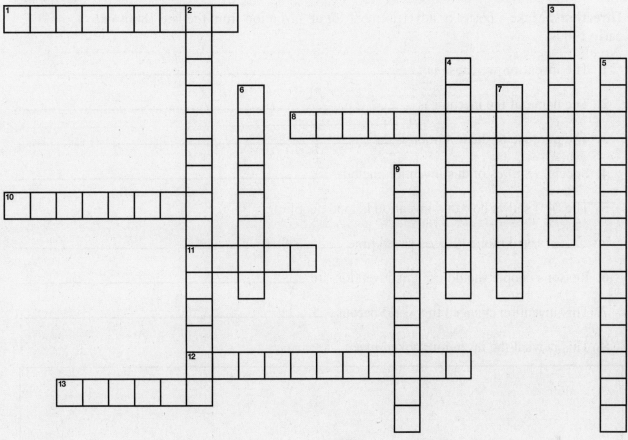

Across

1. unfair negative opinion about a group of people
8. people who work to produce goods and services
10. person who buys or uses goods and services
11. share of a company
12. business that is owned by investors
13. when workers refuse to work to try to force business owners to meet their demands

Down

2. tool or machine that a company can use to produce goods and services
3. variety
4. hot, cramped workshop
5. system in which people are free to start their own businesses and own their own property
6. person who gives to a business or project hoping to gain a profit
7. company that has control of an entire industry
9. group of workers who join together to fight for improved working conditions and better wages

Notes for Home: Your child learned the vocabulary terms for Chapter 4.
Home Activity: Have your child use these words to write a brief summary of what he or she learned in Chapter 4.

UNIT 2 Project Inventions Change the Country

Directions: Make a poster or advertisement for an invention from the late 1800s or early 1900s.

1. The invention we chose is _____.

2. The name of the inventor is _____.

3. The purpose of the invention is _____.

4. Special features of this invention include _____.

5. The (✔) shows how this invention helped people:

   _____ saved money _____ saved time _____ other: _____

6. Reasons people should use this invention are _____.

7. This invention changed the world because _____.

8. This is what the invention looked like:

✔Checklist for Students

_____ We chose an invention from the late 1800s.

_____ We identified the inventor, and we described the invention's purpose, features, and benefits.

_____ We made a poster or advertisement for the invention.

_____ We included a picture of the invention on the poster.

_____ We presented our poster or advertisement to the class.

Notes for Home: Your child researched an invention from the late 1800s and advertised its features to the class.
Home Activity: With your child, identify a modern invention you both agree has changed the world. Discuss how it has impacted your life.

© Scott Foresman / Growth of a Nation

Compare and Contrast

Directions: Read the passage below. Then fill in the circle next to the correct answer.

Following the Civil War, both the North and the South faced adjustments. Soldiers in both regions returned from the battlefield to their homes and jobs. All across the now-reunited country, people faced the terrible reality that thousands would never be returning home. Thousands more, maimed in the fighting, looked forward to an uncertain future.

The South's adjustments, however, were far more complicated than the North's. Unlike the North, which saw little actual fighting, much of the South was a smoking ruin. In addition, the system of slavery no longer existed. This had a dramatic effect on the social and economic systems in the South.

---

1. Which statement best compares the experiences of the North and the South after the Civil War?
   Ⓐ The North faced a more difficult adjustment than the South.
   Ⓑ The South faced a more difficult adjustment than the North.
   Ⓒ Both the North and South faced an adjustment period.
   Ⓓ The South had to deal with the end of slavery.

2. Which statement best contrasts the experiences of the North and the South after the Civil War?
   Ⓐ Both the North and South faced adjustments.
   Ⓑ The South faced a more complicated adjustment than the North.
   Ⓒ Both sides lost many war dead.
   Ⓓ The end of slavery dramatically affected both the North and the South.

3. In the passage, which clue word helps you identify a comparison being made between the North and the South?
   Ⓐ *both*
   Ⓑ *following*
   Ⓒ *unlike*
   Ⓓ *addition*

4. In the passage, which clue word helps you identify a contrast being made between the North and the South?
   Ⓐ *following*
   Ⓑ *unlike*
   Ⓒ *both*
   Ⓓ *no*

 Notes for Home: Your child learned to identify comparisons and contrasts in a passage.
Home Activity: Work with your child to write a two-paragraph description of two buildings in your neighborhood that both compares and contrasts the buildings.

Vocabulary Preview

Directions: Look at the vocabulary words in Chapter 5 of your textbook. Choose the vocabulary word from the chapter that best completes each sentence. Write the word on the line provided.

1. The moving of people from rural areas to cities is _____.

2. A center that provides help for people with little money is a

   _____.

3. Someone who pays rent to use land or buildings that belong to someone else is a

   _____.

4. A _____ is a machine that cuts wheat.

5. A _____ hangs from steel cables.

6. The right to vote is _____.

7. During the _____, about 5 million African Americans moved north.

8. Using machines to do work is called _____.

9. An organization of people that controls votes to gain political power is a

   _____.

10. A building that is divided into small apartments is called a _____.

11. A _____ separates grain from plant stalks.

12. The _____ to the Constitution gave women the right to vote.

13. Before machines were invented, _____ was the only way to get jobs done.

14. To _____ is to give someone the right to vote.

15. A _____ was a person who worked for women's voting rights.

Notes for Home: Your child learned the vocabulary terms for Chapter 5.
Home Activity: Practice saying, spelling, and using these words correctly with your child.

© Scott Foresman / Growth of a Nation

Read Line and Circle Graphs

Directions: Look at the graphs below and answer the questions that follow.

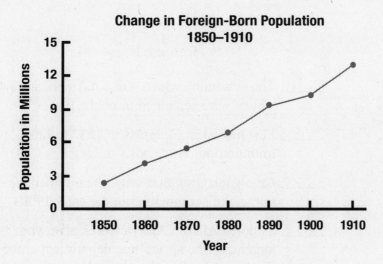

**Change in Foreign-Born Population
1850–1910**

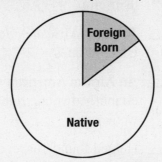

United States Population, 1910

1. Which of these graphs shows the change in population over time?

   _____

2. Which of these graphs tells you how the foreign-born and native populations compare?

   _____

3. Between which years did the United States see the largest increase in its number of foreign-born residents?

   _____

Notes for Home: Your child learned how to read line and circle graphs and how they are different.
Home Activity: Present your child with information—for example, how your family has grown in number over the last 15 years or how many males and females are in your family. Have your child create an appropriate graph of the information you provide.

Lesson 3: Unequal Opportunities

Directions: Write the number of each item in Column A in the blank next to its description in Column B.

Column A

1. sharecropping

2. George Washington Carver

3. racial segregation

4. Homer Plessy

5. Chinese Exclusion Act

6. Jack L. Cooper

7. W. E. B. Du Bois

8. NAACP

9. Booker T. Washington

10. Ida Wells-Barnett

Column B

_____ The system by which African Americans and whites were separated in public places

_____ Law passed in Congress in 1882 to limit immigration on the basis of race

_____ An organization that sought the immediate end to racial discrimination in the early 1900s

_____ A noted African American scientist who organized the agriculture department at the Tuskegee Institute

_____ The system by which African Americans received the use of land in return for a share of their crop

_____ The first African American disc jockey in the United States

_____ An African American who fought segregation and established voting rights for African American women

_____ Helped found Tuskegee Institute and worked to improve the lives of African Americans

_____ Challenged a Jim Crow Law, which helped lead to a famous Supreme Court case of the late 1800s

_____ A writer and editor who helped start the NAACP

Notes for Home: Your child learned about the obstacles to equality for many ethnic groups in the late 1800s and early 1900s, and about the people who worked to overcome those obstacles.
Home Activity: Discuss racial prejudice with your child. Ask whether he or she thinks conditions today have improved or gotten worse since the early 1900s.

Lesson 4: Women's Rights

Directions: Using information from this lesson, circle the term in parentheses that best completes each sentence.

1. In the 1800s, women's opportunities and rights (did, did not) equal those of men.

2. In 1848, women's rights leaders Lucretia Mott and Elizabeth Cady Stanton invited people to gather in (Seneca Falls, New York; Argonia, Kansas) to discuss women's rights.

3. The most controversial idea of the convention was that women should be able to (vote, own property).

4. Suffragist (Lucy Stone, Carrie Chapman Catt) founded the American Woman Suffrage Association in 1870.

5. Women came closer to having equality in (urban, rural) areas.

6. The first woman mayor in the United States was (Susannah Medora Salter, Susan B. Anthony).

7. (Susan B. Anthony, Marguerite Harrison), who worked for women's rights until her death in 1906, said that "There will never be complete equality until women themselves help to make laws and elect lawmakers."

8. By 1912, (many, no) states had approved a woman's right to vote.

9. World War I helped (strengthen, weaken) the cause of women's suffrage.

10. In 1919, Congress passed the (Nineteenth, Fifteenth) Amendment, which gave women the right to vote.

© Scott Foresman / Growth of a Nation

Notes for Home: Your child learned about the changes in women's roles and rights in the 1800s and early 1900s.
Home Activity: With your child, look at a newspaper or magazine and note every time you see a story that includes a woman holding a job, political office, or other position of authority.

Name _____ Date _____

Vocabulary Review

Directions: Match each vocabulary term to its meaning. Write the letter of the word on the blank next to its meaning.

_____ 1. large-scale movement of African Americans from the South to the North in the early 1900s

_____ 2. movement of people from rural areas to cities

_____ 3. using machines to do work

_____ 4. the right to vote

_____ 5. machine that cuts wheat

_____ 6. gave women right to vote

_____ 7. someone who pays rent for land or buildings

_____ 8. building divided into small apartments

_____ 9. person who fought to win suffrage

_____ 10. to give someone the right to vote

_____ 11. machine for separating grain from its stalk

_____ 12. a place where needy people receive assistance

_____ 13. work performed by hand

_____ 14. bridge supported by steel cables

_____ 15. organization of people who control votes to gain power

a. manual labor

b. mechanization

c. reaper

d. threshing machine

e. urbanization

f. tenement

g. settlement house

h. political machine

i. suspension bridge

j. tenant

k. enfranchise

l. Great Migration

m. suffrage

n. suffragist

o. Nineteenth Amendment

Notes for Home: Your child learned the vocabulary terms for Chapter 5.
Home Activity: Discuss the vocabulary terms and how they relate to people and events in the news.

Vocabulary Preview

Directions: Choose the vocabulary word from Chapter 6 that best completes each sentence. Write the word on the line provided. You may use your textbook.

1. Theodore Roosevelt organized the _____ to fight in Cuba.

2. The _____ heavily punished the Germans for their role in World War I.

3. In an effort to control people's behavior, leaders passed _____.

4. Because of its _____ with Belgium, Great Britain entered World War I.

5. _____, or exaggerated reporting, whipped up public anger against Spain.

6. Upton Sinclair was a well-known _____ who uncovered the truth about meat packing plants.

7. The United States never joined President Wilson's _____.

8. The United States emerged from the _____ as a world power.

9. The _____ fought Native Americans before fighting in Cuba.

10. John Muir encouraged _____ of the nation's scenic places.

11. The United States planned to build the canal at the _____ of Panama.

12. The _____ Era was dedicated to reform.

13. Standard Oil was a powerful _____ of the late 1800s.

14. _____ was a contributing factor in World War I.

15. The great conflict that swept Europe starting in 1914 was called _____.

16. One reason the United States did not enter World War I at first was a strong feeling of _____ in the country.

Notes for Home: Your child learned the vocabulary terms for Chapter 6.
Home Activity: Make flip cards to quiz your child on the meaning of these terms.

© Scott Foresman / Growth of a Nation

Lesson 1: Expanding Overseas

Directions: Using information from this lesson, circle the term in parentheses that best completes each sentence.

1. William Seward sought to expand the territory of the United States through the purchase of (Alaska, Hawaii).

2. Alaska proved to be a valuable addition to the United States after the discovery of (salmon, gold).

3. American planters in Hawaii wanted the United States to (free, annex) the islands.

4. Many people in the United States were (pleased, angered) by Spain's reaction to the Cuban revolution of 1895.

5. The destruction of the *Maine* and yellow journalism reports about it helped tip public opinion (in favor of, against) war with Spain.

6. Commodore George Dewey led the attack on the Spanish Fleet in (the Philippines, Cuba).

7. Theodore Roosevelt helped organize a force known as the (Buffalo Soldiers, Rough Riders).

8. The Spanish-American War showed that the United States was a (powerful, weak) nation.

9. Theodore Roosevelt emerged from the war as a (villain, hero).

10. (Mosquitoes, The Panamanian people) were a major obstacle to building the Panama Canal.

© Scott Foresman / Growth of a Nation

Notes for Home: Your child learned about the emergence of the United States as a major world power.
Home Activity: With your child, review a newspaper or Internet news site for stories about the United States and its role in international affairs today.

Credibility of a Source

Some sources of information are more believable than others. This is due, in part, to who is presenting the information.

Directions: Read the two passages about General George Armstrong Custer and answer the questions that follow.

Passage A comes from a historical novel. The story is presented as a part-fact, part-fiction presentation of Custer's journal. As you read the words, imagine them to be directly from Custer, himself.

> *Perhaps I have worshiped my superiors too well with not enough thought of myself. [My wife,] Libbie, says that I have always been too hasty in putting the needs of others ahead of my own.*

Passage B comes from a biography. It is based on fact. At times the author includes a personal point of view or conclusion, as well as reports from others who were involved in the actual situation.

> *What [Custer] did was perfectly in keeping with his nature. He did what he had always done: push ahead, disregard orders, start a fight. . . .*
>
> *So he marched his men most of the night and flung them into battle when—as a number of Native Americans noted—they were so tired their legs shook when they dismounted.*

1. According to Passage A, how did Custer treat his superiors? According to Passage B?

   _____

   _____

2. According to Passage A, how did Custer treat others, in general? According to Passage B?

   _____

   _____

   _____

3. Which passage has more credibility? Why?

   _____

   _____

   _____

   _____

Notes for Home: Your child learned how to determine the credibility of a source.
Home Activity: With your child, brainstorm various sources of information and discuss the credibility of each.

Lesson 2: The Progressive Movement

Directions: Answer the following questions on the lines provided. You may use your textbook.

1. What kinds of problems did the growth of industry create in the United States?

_____

_____

_____

2. What were trusts?

_____

_____

_____

3. Who were the Progressives and what were their goals?

_____

_____

_____

4. Who were the muckrakers and how did they get their name?

_____

_____

_____

5. Who was John Muir, and what role did he play in the Progressive Movement?

_____

_____

_____

Notes for Home: Your child learned about the key individuals and issues of the Progressive Movement in the United States.
Home Activity: Discuss the word *Progressive* and what it means. Talk with your child about whether there is a continuing need for Progressive-type activities in the United States.

Interpret Political Cartoons

A political cartoon is a drawing that shows people or events in the news in a way that makes you smile or laugh. The goal of political cartoons is to make you think about events.

Directions: Use this cartoon about women's rights to answer the questions below.

"MAKE WAY!"

1. Where do the women appear in this cartoon? What are they doing? Why do you think the cartoonist portrayed these characters as she did?

   _____

   _____

   _____

   _____

   _____

   _____

2. What do you think the signs in the cartoon represent?

   _____

3. In this cartoon, men are being pushed off the world. What do you think this means?

   _____

   _____

4. A woman named Laura Foster drew this political cartoon. How do you think she felt about women's rights? Explain.

   _____

   _____

   _____

Notes for Home: Your child learned how to interpret political cartoons.
Home Activity: With your child, look through recent newspapers or magazines to find a political cartoon. Discuss the cartoon's message and the cartoonist's point of view.

Lesson 3: World War I

Directions: Complete the chart with information from this lesson. You may use your textbook.

Cause	Effect
	Increased tension in Europe, formation of alliances
	Casualty figures rise shockingly
United States pursues policy of isolationism	
United States enters the fighting	
	United States does not join League of Nations

Notes for Home: Your child learned about the causes and events of World War I.
Home Activity: Read a newspaper article about an armed conflict taking place in the world today. Discuss the terrible sacrifices that war requires of the people involved.

Directions: Suppose that you are a pilot during World War I. Write a diary entry in which you describe your flying gear, your aircraft, and your experiences as you fly over enemy territory.

_____

_____

_____

_____

_____

_____

_____

_____

_____

_____

_____

_____

_____

_____

_____

_____

_____

_____

_____

_____

Notes for Home: Your child learned how airplanes changed the way war was fought during World War I.
Home Activity: Discuss with your child how technological advances have changed the way war is fought today.

Vocabulary Review

Directions: Use each of the vocabulary terms from Chapter 6 in a sentence. Write the sentences on the lines provided. You may use your glossary.

Rough Riders	yellow journalism	Spanish-American War	Progressive
Treaty of Versailles	muckrakers	Buffalo Soldiers	trust
Blue Laws	League of Nations	conservation	nationalism
alliance		isthmus	isolationism
			World War I

1. _____

2. _____

3. _____

4. _____

5. _____

6. _____

7. _____

8. _____

9. _____

10. _____

11. _____

12. _____

13. _____

14. _____

15. _____

16. _____

Notes for Home: Your child learned the vocabulary terms from Chapter 6.
Home Activity: Practice saying, spelling, and using these terms correctly in an oral discussion with your child.

UNIT 3 Project Arts and Letters

Create an infomercial about an important invention. Form a group, choose an invention studied in this unit, and research the invention.

1. The invention we chose is _____.

2. Below is some information about the invention. The ✔ shows my role in the infomercial.

____ **Business or product representative:** Describe the invention and its history. Then describe the inventor and why he or she made the invention.

_____

____ **Satisfied customer:** Tell about your experience with the invention and why you recommend it.

_____

____ **Local resident or official:** Tell how the invention is different from other products and how it has helped people and made their lives easier.

_____

✔ Checklist for Students

____ We chose an invention from the unit.

____ We found information about our invention.

____ We wrote a script for our infomercial.

____ We made a poster or banner to use in our infomercial.

____ We presented our infomercial to the class.

Notes for Home: Your child researched an invention and helped present an infomercial to the class.
Home Activity: Discuss with your child what inventions in your household are most important to your everyday lives.

Draw Conclusions

Directions: A conclusion is a judgment a person makes based on facts or details. Read the information below. Then answer the questions that follow. Fill in the circle next to the correct answer.

> The late 1800s and early 1900s brought a variety of new inventions to the United States. These inventions forever changed life as people knew it. For example, when electricity became widely available, new electric appliances were invented. People were able to use electric washing machines, irons, upright vacuum cleaners, and sewing machines. Household chores could be done quickly and more easily than ever before. After the invention of the telephone, telephone poles and lines went up all over the country. People could communicate over great distances without leaving their homes or businesses. The invention of the automobile and the creation of better roads had an enormous impact on American life. Farmers had reliable transportation for taking their crops to market. People could live away from their jobs and drive long distances to vacation.

1. Which statement best supports the conclusion that new inventions gave people more free time at home?

   Ⓐ After the invention of the telephone, telephone poles and lines went up all over the country.

   Ⓑ Household chores could be done quickly and more easily than ever before.

   Ⓒ Farmers had reliable transportation for taking their crops to market.

   Ⓓ People could live away from their jobs and drive long distances to vacation.

2. Which statement best supports the conclusion that the invention of the car affected where people decided to make their homes?

   Ⓐ People took vacations in their cars.

   Ⓑ Better roads were needed for all the new cars.

   Ⓒ Farmers used automobiles to take their crops to market.

   Ⓓ People could live away from their jobs and drive to work.

3. What conclusion might you draw after reading the information above?

   Ⓐ People were happy to be able to call their neighbors on the telephone and visit their neighbors by car, but they probably preferred to do household chores by hand.

   Ⓑ A variety of new inventions made life much more difficult for many Americans.

   Ⓒ New inventions gave people more time and freedom and helped people to communicate with each other.

   Ⓓ It was challenging to take care of all the new roads, telephone lines, and appliances that suddenly appeared all over the country.

Notes for Home: Your child learned how to use facts and details to draw conclusions.
Home Activity: Read a newspaper article with your child. Help your child use facts or details presented in the article to draw conclusions about the subject.

© Scott Foresman / Growth of a Nation

Vocabulary Preview

Directions: Use the vocabulary words from Chapter 7 to complete each item. Use the numbered letters to answer the clue that follows.

1. rapid rise in prices

— — — — — — — — —
    1

2. program that provides monthly payments to the elderly, disabled, and unemployed

— — — — — — — — — — — — — — — —
        14

3. public forms of communication that reach large audiences

— — — — — — — — —
         2

4. area of the Great Plains affected by dust storms

— — — — — — — —
  13

5. amendment that outlawed the making, sale, and transporting of alcoholic beverages

t 8 t h A d r e n n
7

e l l — — — — — — —

6. system in which workers stand in one place and put parts together as the pieces go by on a moving belt

a s s e m b l y l i n e
           11

7. programs to help the country out of the Great Depression

— — — — — — — —
18

8. musical form that was influenced by African American traditions

J a z z
  19

9. long period without rain

d r o u g h t
    4

Vocabulary Preview (continued)

10. the condition of being out of work

— —₉ — — — — — — — — —

11. the making of large quantities of goods that are exactly alike

— — — — —₅ — — — — — — — —

12. a worker who moves from place to place to harvest crops

— — — —₈ — — — — — — —

13. amendment that ended Prohibition

— —₃ — — — — —

—₁₇ — — — — — —

14. place where stocks are bought and sold

—₁₅ — — — — — — — —

15. period in which artists used writing, music, and painting to share their ideas and feelings about life for African Americans

— — — —₆ — — — — — — — — —

16. ban on the sale of alcohol

— — — — — — — — —₁₂ —

17. worst period of economic hardship in United States history

— — — — — — — — — — —₁₀ — — —

18. borrowed money

— — — — —₁₆ —

Clue: Birthplace of jazz

—₁ —₂ —₃ —₄ —₅ —₆ —₇ —₈ —₉ —₁₀,

—₁₁ —₁₂ —₁₃ —₁₄ —₁₅ —₁₆ —₁₇ —₁₈ —₁₉

Notes for Home: Your child learned the vocabulary words from Chapter 7.
Home Activity: Practice saying, spelling, and using these words correctly with your child.

© Scott Foresman / Growth of a Nation

Lesson 1: An Industrial Nation

Directions: Complete the outline with information from this lesson. You may use
your textbook.

I. Nation of Drivers

A. _____ wanted to make a car that was sturdy, safe,

and affordable. The _____, which was produced on an
assembly line, cost less than half the amount of other cars.

B. The growing number of cars led to a demand for _____
and created many new jobs.

II. Age of Radio

A. Before it was viewed as a form of entertainment, radio was used for communication

between _____. The first radio message across the Atlantic

Ocean was sent by _____.

B. Others saw the potential for commercial radio.

   1. _____ developed a transmitter that made amateur
broadcasts.

   2. _____ became the first professional radio station
in the world.

   3. _____ brought his ideas for broadcasting music,
news, entertainment, and sports to the Radio Corporation of America.

III. Rise of the Movie Industry

A. Movies became a popular form of inexpensive entertainment.

   1. Most movies were made in _____, part of Los
Angeles, California.

   2. In 1927, new technology allowed movies to include _____.

Notes for Home: Your child learned how new technology changed American culture in the early 1900s.
Home Activity: Ask your child how technology affects American culture today.

Fact and Opinion

Directions: A fact is a statement that can be checked and proved to be true. An opinion is a personal view that cannot be proved to be true or false. Read the excerpts that follow. Look for facts and opinions. Underline the facts and circle the opinions.

> The increase in automobiles in the mid-1900s helped create many new jobs. The most important jobs were in factories, where people built cars. People also repaired roads and opened car repair shops, hotels, gas stations, and restaurants for travelers.
>
> In the early 1900s, movies quickly became a popular form of inexpensive entertainment. People lined up to see movies, and some people copied the clothing and hairstyles of their favorite movie stars. I think life in the United States was probably boring before the invention of movies!
>
> The first professional radio station in the world began broadcasting in 1920 from Pittsburgh, Pennsylvania. It was the best thing that could have happened to the people of the United States. Listeners could hear news reports, sporting events, comedies, dramas, and music programs.

Directions: In the spaces provided, write one fact and one opinion about mass media in the United States in the early 1900s.

Fact

_____

_____

_____

Opinion

_____

_____

_____

Notes for Home: Your child learned to distinguish between fact and opinion.
Home Activity: Read a movie review with your child. Work together to identify the facts and opinions presented by the writer.

© Scott Foresman / Growth of a Nation

Lesson 2: The Roaring Twenties

Directions: Complete the chart with information from this lesson. Tell how each person was a part of the changing United States during the 1920s. You may use your textbook.

Duke Ellington	
Louis Armstrong	
Bessie Smith	
F. Scott Fitzgerald	
Langston Hughes	
Zora Neale Hurston	
Jacob Lawrence	
Charles Lindbergh	
Amelia Earhart	
Georgia O'Keeffe	

© Scott Foresman / Growth of a Nation

Notes for Home: Your child learned about the changes in culture and the roles of women during the 1920s.
Home Activity: Help your child use library or Internet resources to learn more about an individual studied in this lesson. Work with your child to write a brief biographical entry about this person.

Lesson 3: The Good Times End

Directions: Complete the chart with information from this lesson. Identify five causes and five effects of the Great Depression. You may use your textbook.

Causes

Effects

Notes for Home: Your child learned about the causes and effects of the Great Depression.
Home Activity: Discuss with your child what it might have been like to live through the Great Depression. Discuss the hardships you and your family might have faced.

Lesson 4: The New Deal

Directions: Write the number of each item in Column A next to its description in Column B.

Column A	**Column B**
1. Franklin D. Roosevelt	_____ provided monthly benefits to the elderly, disabled, and unemployed
2. Farm Security Administration	_____ site of the 1939 World's Fair
3. Securities and Exchange Commission	_____ described the hardships faced by migrant workers in *The Grapes of Wrath*
4. Social Security	_____ took photographs that showed how the Great Depression affected people
5. Civilian Conservation Corps	_____ set up work camps for unemployed young men
6. Dodge City, Kansas	_____ traveled the country to see if New Deal programs were improving conditions
7. John Steinbeck	_____ helped farmers buy needed equipment
8. Eleanor Roosevelt	_____ promised "a new deal for the American people"
9. Dorothea Lange	_____ area affected by the Dust Bowl
10. Queens, New York	_____ set up to protect investors in the stock market

Directions: Suppose that you are a farmer in an area affected by the Dust Bowl in the 1930s. Write a brief diary entry describing the hardships you and your family face.

_____

_____

_____

_____

_____

_____

_____

_____

Notes for Home: Your child learned about the government's efforts to help the country through the Great Depression and the difficult times that continued throughout the 1930s.
Home Activity: Ask your child his or her point of view on how big a role the government should play in people's lives.

Vocabulary Review

Directions: Read each sentence. Match the underlined vocabulary term with its definition below. Write the words on the lines provided.

Ford's Model Ts were built using an <u>assembly line</u>.

<u>Mass production</u> was used to manufacture many different products.

Radio joined newspapers as a form of <u>mass media</u>.

People who opposed <u>Prohibition</u> argued that the government should not be allowed to control how people behaved.

Reformers who supported Prohibition helped pass the <u>Eighteenth Amendment</u>.

The <u>Twenty-first Amendment</u> to the Constitution was adopted in 1933.

Duke Ellington, Louis Armstrong, and Bessie Smith were popular <u>jazz</u> performers during the 1920s.

Langston Hughes and Zora Neale Hurston were popular <u>Harlem Renaissance</u> writers.

Rising <u>unemployment</u> in the late 1920s meant fewer people could afford to buy new products.

---

1. amendment that ended Prohibition _____

2. musical form that was influenced by African American traditions

   _____

3. the condition of being out of work _____

4. amendment that outlawed the making, sale, and transporting of alcoholic beverages

   _____

5. system in which workers stand in one place and put parts together as the pieces go by on a

   moving belt _____

6. period in which artists used writing, music, and painting to share their ideas and feelings

   about life for African Americans _____

7. ban on the sale of alcohol _____

8. the making of large quantities of goods that are exactly alike

   _____

9. public forms of communication that reach large audiences

   _____

Vocabulary Review (continued)

The center of the <u>stock market</u> is the New York Stock Exchange on Wall Street.

Many people were without jobs during the <u>Great Depression</u>.

One reason why the stock market crash of 1929 caused panic was that many investors had bought their stocks on <u>credit</u>.

President Roosevelt's <u>New Deal</u> focused on relief, recovery, and reform.

Some New Deal programs, such as <u>Social Security</u>, are still in effect today.

A severe <u>drought</u> hit the Great Plains in the 1930s.

The worst storm of the <u>Dust Bowl</u> affected parts of Kansas, Colorado, Texas, and Oklahoma.

Many farmers affected by the Dust Bowl moved west and became <u>migrant workers</u>.

<u>Inflation</u> soared in Germany, causing German money to become worthless.

10. long period without rain _____

11. rapid rise in prices _____

12. programs to help the country out of the Great Depression

_____

13. place where stocks are bought and sold _____

14. program that provides monthly payments to the elderly, disabled, and unemployed

_____

15. area of the Great Plains affected by dust storms _____

16. a worker who moves from place to place to harvest crops _____

17. borrowed money _____

18. worst period of economic hardship in United States history

_____

Notes for Home: Your child learned the vocabulary words for Chapter 7.
Home Activity: Ask your child to summarize what he or she learned in Chapter 7 using these words.

Vocabulary Preview

Directions: Preview the vocabulary in Chapter 8 of your textbook. Then match each vocabulary term below to its meaning. Write the letter of the term on the blank next to its meaning.

_____ 1. policy through which the United States would let Britain borrow all the military supplies it needed to fight the Axis

_____ 2. work camps in which many Jews and others were imprisoned during World War II

_____ 3. form of government in which individual freedoms are denied

_____ 4. fight for a major city in the Soviet Union

_____ 5. alliance formed by Germany, Italy, and Japan

_____ 6. group of African American fighter pilots

_____ 7. alliance formed by Britain and France

_____ 8. the murder of millions of Jews in Europe by the Nazis

_____ 9. battle that took place near a small island located northwest of Hawaii

_____ 10. leader who gains complete control of a country's government

_____ 11. biggest battle ever fought by the United States Army

_____ 12. major war that began when Britain and France declared war on Germany

_____ 13. code name for the effort to build an atomic bomb

_____ 14. limiting the amount of food each person in the United States could buy

_____ 15. weapon that would create massive explosive energy by splitting atoms

a. Allies

b. atomic bomb

c. Axis

d. Battle of Midway

e. Battle of Stalingrad

f. Battle of the Bulge

g. concentration camps

h. dictator

i. fascism

j. Holocaust

k. Lend-Lease

l. Manhattan Project

m. rationing

n. Tuskegee Airmen

o. World War II

Notes for Home: Your child learned the vocabulary words from Chapter 8.
Home Activity: Practice saying, spelling, and using these words correctly with your child.

Lesson 1: World War II Begins

Directions: Sequence the events below in the order in which they took place by numbering them 1–10. You may use your textbook.

_____ Britain and France, known as the Allies, warn Hitler not to invade Poland. Hitler ignores this threat.

_____ The U.S. House of Representatives and Senate vote to declare war on Japan.

_____ Nearly all of Western Europe, including France, eventually falls to the Germans. Britain stands alone in Europe in the fight against the Axis.

_____ Japanese planes bomb the United States naval base at Pearl Harbor.

_____ Germany and Italy declare war on the United States, and the United States joins the war as one of the Allies.

_____ There is a rise of dictators in Europe and Asia. Dictators Hitler and Mussolini sign a treaty agreeing to support each other.

_____ Britain and France declare war on Germany.

_____ The United States begins drafting men into the military.

_____ Germany, Italy, and Japan become known as the Axis and begin invading countries throughout the world.

_____ President Roosevelt does not send United States troops into the war, but decides to lend Britain military supplies.

Directions: Respond to the following prompt on the lines provided.

Explain the reasons why many people in the United States at first supported isolationism during World War II. Then explain why these feelings toward isolationism began to change.

_____

_____

_____

_____

_____

_____

_____

Notes for Home: Your child learned about the events leading up to World War II.
Home Activity: With your child, look at a world map or a globe and locate the countries that were involved in World War II. Discuss how you both feel about the decision of the United States to stay out of the war and then its decision to enter the war.

Lesson 2: The Home Front

Directions: Describe each of the following people, places, and terms and tell how they relate to life for Americans during World War II.

1. Women's Army Corps

_____

_____

_____

2. Benjamin O. Davis, Jr.

_____

_____

_____

3. Japanese Americans and Executive Order #9066

_____

_____

_____

_____

4. Albert Einstein

_____

_____

_____

5. Los Alamos, New Mexico

_____

_____

_____

Notes for Home: Your child learned about how World War II affected life in the United States.
Home Activity: Role play with your child. Take turns talking about the effects of the war on life in the United States from the point of view of a factory worker, a woman, a Japanese American, and an African American pilot.

Lesson 3: The World at War

Directions: Write *True* or *False* next to each statement. If the statement is false, rewrite it on the lines provided to make it true. You may use your textbook.

1. Admiral Chester Nimitz was a commander of the United States naval forces in the Pacific at the time of the Battle of Midway, a turning point in the war.

_____

_____

2. Dwight D. Eisenhower was in command of the Allied forces when they invaded Hiroshima, Japan, in 1944.

_____

_____

3. General George S. Patton and his United States troops suffered heavy losses and eventually defeat at the Battle of the Bulge.

_____

_____

4. President Harry S. Truman was encouraged to use atomic bombs against Japan, but he was unwilling to do so.

_____

_____

Directions: Answer the following questions on the lines provided.

What was the Holocaust? Who was Anne Frank?

_____

_____

_____

_____

_____

_____

Notes for Home: Your child learned about major events of World War II and how the United States helped lead the Allies to victory.
Home Activity: Ask your child to explain what he or she learned about the role of the United States in World War II. Which event of the war did he or she find most interesting or disturbing?

Name _____ Date _____

Understand Key Lines of Latitude and Longitude

Directions: Review the map below. Then answer the questions on the lines provided.

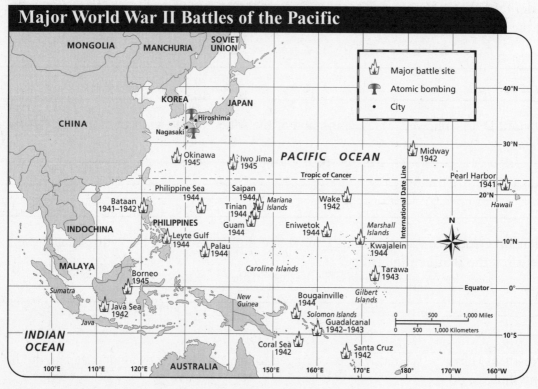

Major World War II Battles of the Pacific

1. What is the International Date Line? Where is it located?

_____

_____

_____

2. Which battle took place approximately ten degrees west of the International Date Line, at latitude 10°S?

_____

3. At what approximate latitude and longitude did each of the following battles take place?

Pearl Harbor _____

Bataan _____

Notes for Home: Your child learned to use latitude and longitude to locate places on a map.
Home Activity: With your child, use a map of the United States to find your state and the general location of your city or town. Help your child to identify the approximate latitude and longitude of these areas.

Vocabulary Review

Directions: Write each vocabulary word from Chapter 8 beside the clues listed below. You may use your textbook.

_____ 1. Code name for a bomb project

_____ 2. Germany, Italy, and Japan

_____ 3. Creates explosive energy by splitting atoms

_____ 4. Place where Jews and others were imprisoned by Hitler

_____ 5. Fight for a city in the Soviet Union

_____ 6. Britain and France

_____ 7. System that denies individual freedoms

_____ 8. Biggest World War II battle for the United States

_____ 9. Policy of letting Britain borrow war supplies

_____ 10. Limiting food purchases

_____ 11. Major war in Europe and Asia

_____ 12. Battle northwest of Hawaii

_____ 13. Murder of millions of Jews

_____ 14. African American fighter pilots

_____ 15. Leader with complete control of a government

Notes for Home: Your child learned the vocabulary words from Chapter 8.
Home Activity: Discuss with your child how each term relates to important events of World War II.

Use with Page 374.

UNIT 4 Project Feature Movie

In this unit, you learned about history's real-life athletes and pilots. Bring one of these people to the screen by creating a feature movie about his or her achievements. Form a group and choose the athlete or pilot from this unit that you find most interesting.

1. The person we chose is: _____.

2. Here is a brief summary of his or her accomplishments: _____

_____

_____

_____

_____

3. The ✔ shows what jobs I will have in creating the movie:

___ writer   ___ actor

___ set designer   ___ sound effects/music coordinator

Notes _____

_____

_____

✔ Checklist for Students

____ We chose an athlete or pilot from Unit 4.

____ We wrote a screenplay or script for a short movie based on the person's accomplishments.

____ We wrote dialogue for the characters and instructions for camera operators.

____ We wrote about the location and setting for the movie and created a backdrop for the screenplay.

____ We performed the movie for the class.

Notes for Home: Your child worked with his or her classmates to create a movie based on the accomplishments of an athlete or pilot from this unit.
Home Activity: Have your child describe the movie he or she presented in class today. Be sure your child shares why the person featured in the movie is interesting to him or her.

© Scott Foresman / Growth of a Nation

Cause and Effect

Directions: A cause is why something happens. An effect is what happens. Identifying cause-and-effect relationships can help you gain a better understanding of what you read. Read the paragraph below. Then answer the questions that follow.

The years after World War II are often referred to as "boom years" because of the economic growth and prosperity the country experienced during this time. During the war, many families had to make sacrifices. Goods were rationed because the nation's industries were focused on producing war supplies. With family wage earners helping the war effort abroad, those at home had to get by with less. When the war finally came to an end, reunited families looked forward to a bright future. Americans began spending money like never before, which caused businesses and industries to grow. Many families looked outside of crowded cities to buy new homes. As a result, suburbs began to grow rapidly all over the country. The number of babies born in the years after the war also soared, resulting in the largest generation in the country's history. In the years ahead, these "boom years" would affect the nation in many ways.

1. Why are the years after World War II sometimes called "boom years"?

    Ⓐ Many families had to make sacrifices.
    Ⓑ Goods needed to be rationed.
    Ⓒ The country experienced economic growth and prosperity.
    Ⓓ Family wage earners were helping the war effort abroad.

2. Why were goods rationed during the war?

    Ⓐ People were spending money like never before.
    Ⓑ Industries were focused on producing war supplies.
    Ⓒ Cities became too crowded.
    Ⓓ Suburbs were growing rapidly.

3. Which of the following was an effect of Americans' increased spending?

    Ⓐ Businesses and industries grew.
    Ⓑ Many babies were born.
    Ⓒ Many had to get by with less.
    Ⓓ Reunited families looked forward to a bright future.

4. What was an effect of families' desire to move out of crowded cities?

    Ⓐ Cities grew rapidly   Ⓒ Businesses grew rapidly.
    Ⓑ Suburbs grew rapidly.   Ⓓ Industries grew rapidly.

Notes for Home: Your child learned to identify cause-and-effect relationships.
Home Activity: Have your child list several important life events. Then work together to identify the causes and effects of these events.

Vocabulary Preview

Directions: Match each vocabulary word with its meaning. Write the vocabulary word on the line next to its meaning. You may use your glossary.

aggressor	communism	Berlin Airlift	suburbs
Marshall Plan	ideology	Cold War	
United Nations	NATO	propaganda	

1. _____ residential districts outside a city

2. _____ political and economic system in which the government owns all the businesses and land

3. _____ person or nation that starts a war

4. _____ beliefs

5. _____ military alliance between the United States and the nations of Western Europe

6. _____ when airplanes flew food and fuel into West Berlin

7. _____ organization of 50 countries established to promote global cooperation

8. _____ a systematic effort to spread opinions or beliefs

9. _____ program for European recovery after World War II

10. _____ long, bitter struggle between the United States and the Soviet Union

Vocabulary Preview (continued)

AFL-CIO	commute	arms race	Berlin Wall
G.I. Bill of Rights	Korean War	Cuban Missile Crisis	
consumer credit	credit card	Red Scare	

11. _____ conflict in which the Soviets were setting up nuclear missiles in Cuba

12. _____ race to build more and better weapons than an enemy

13. _____ panic about communists

14. _____ credit that is used to buy goods that are consumed

15. _____ card that allows the card owner to charge goods and services and then pay off the charge

16. _____ trip to work

17. _____ law that provided benefits to help veterans succeed in civilian society

18. _____ wall that prevented people in East Berlin from fleeing to non-communist West Berlin

19. _____ conflict in which United Nations forces defended South Korea against North Korean invasions

20. _____ largest labor organization in the nation

Notes for Home: Your child learned the vocabulary words from Chapter 9.
Home Activity: Practice saying, spelling, and using these words correctly with your child.

© Scott Foresman / Growth of a Nation

Lesson 1: The World Is Divided

Directions: Complete the cause-and-effect chart with information from this lesson. You may use your textbook.

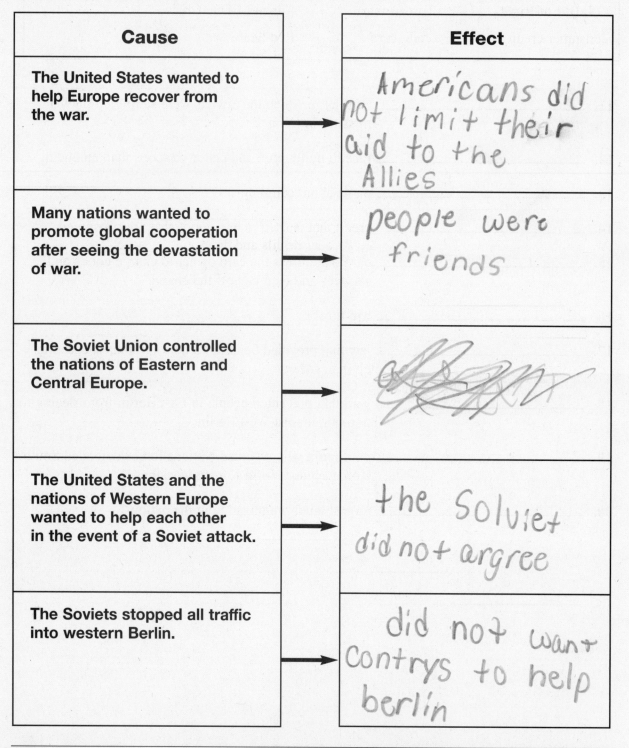

Cause	Effect
The United States wanted to help Europe recover from the war.	Americans did not limit their aid to the Allies
Many nations wanted to promote global cooperation after seeing the devastation of war.	people were friends
The Soviet Union controlled the nations of Eastern and Central Europe.	*(scribbled out)*
The United States and the nations of Western Europe wanted to help each other in the event of a Soviet attack.	the Solviet did not argree
The Soviets stopped all traffic into western Berlin.	did not want contrys to help berlin

Notes for Home: Your child learned about the struggle between free western nations and the communist countries controlled by the Soviet Union in the years after World War II.
Home Activity: Talk with your child about the many nations today that harbor vastly different ideologies. Discuss how these differences play a role in foreign relations.

© Scott Foresman / Growth of a Nation

Compare Primary and Secondary Sources

Directions: Primary sources are eyewitness accounts. Secondary sources are secondhand accounts. Primary and secondary sources can provide different points of view of the same information. Answer the following questions about primary and secondary sources.

1. What are some examples of primary sources?

   _____

   _____

2. What are some examples of secondary sources?

   _____

   _____

3. Which type of source often includes broader details and draws on multiple sources of information?

   _____

   _____

4. Which type of source gives a firsthand account of an event and can offer emotion and vivid descriptions?

   _____

   _____

5. Suppose you wanted to read more about the Cold War in a single source. What type of source do you think would be the most helpful? Explain.

   _____

   _____

   _____

   _____

© Scott Foresman / Growth of a Nation

Notes for Home: Your child learned to compare primary and secondary sources.
Home Activity: Help your child locate a primary source written about a historical event of interest. Then find a secondary source about the same event. Discuss the differences in perspective each source offers.

Lesson 2: Boom Years at Home

Directions: Complete the outline with information from this lesson. You may use your textbook.

The Boom Years

I. The Economy

   A. Americans began spending more after the war.

      1. _____ and industries grew.

   B. Many families wanted to buy new homes.

      1. _____ could soon be found all over the country.

II. The Workplace

   A. War veterans returned to work.

   B. A growing number of occupations were represented by _____.

      1. Many workers were able to work _____ hours.

      2. The _____ became the largest labor organization in the country.

III. The Role of Women

   A. More and more women entered the work force.

      1. By 1960, _____ of American women worked outside the home.

IV. Daily Life

   A. Many Americans enjoyed more _____ time.

   B. The number of children in the United States increased from 47.3 million to _____ between 1950 and 1960.

   C. New highways met the needs of men and women who had to _____ to work.

V. Technology

   A. Improvements were made in transportation.

   B. The television became a standard household appliance.

   C. Homes became more comfortable with better heating and new _____ systems.

Notes for Home: Your child learned about the changing United States in the years following World War II.
Home Activity: Ask your child to identify some ways that the United States has changed in his or her lifetime.

© Scott Foresman / Growth of a Nation

Name _____ Date _____

Lesson 3: Cold War Conflicts

Directions: Explain each term and tell how it relates to the Cold War. Write your answers on the lines provided.

1. Korean War

_____

_____

_____

_____

2. Red Scare

_____

_____

_____

3. Arms race

_____

_____

_____

_____

4. Cuban Missile Crisis

_____

_____

_____

5. Berlin Wall

_____

_____

_____

_____

© Scott Foresman / Growth of a Nation

Notes for Home: Your child learned about the increasing Cold War tensions during the 1950s and 1960s.
Home Activity: Discuss with your child how these tensions affected daily life for Americans.

Vocabulary Review

Directions: Choose the vocabulary word from the box that best completes each sentence. Write the word on the line provided.

credit card	arms race	suburbs	AFL-CIO
Marshall Plan	Berlin Wall	Cold War	
communism	NATO	Cuban Missile Crisis	

1. The _____ became the largest labor organization in the nation.

2. The members of _____ promised to help each other in the event of a Soviet attack.

3. A _____ allows the card owner to charge goods and services.

4. In the system of _____, the government owns all the businesses and land.

5. The _____ separated East Berlin from West Berlin.

6. The _____ was a long, bitter struggle.

7. The _____ was a program for European recovery.

8. The United States and the Soviet Union competed in an _____ to build more and better weapons.

9. Residential districts outside a city are called _____.

10. During the _____, President Kennedy insisted that the Soviets remove their missiles from Cuba.

Vocabulary Review (continued)

United Nations	aggressor	Berlin Airlift	commute
ideology	Red Scare	consumer credit	
Korean War	propaganda	G.I. Bill of Rights	

11. The _____ provided benefits to help veterans succeed.

12. _____ is credit that is used to buy goods that are consumed.

13. Many people who moved to the suburbs had to _____ to work.

14. The _____ is an organization of 50 countries that promotes global cooperation.

15. The Americans and British organized the _____ to deliver food and fuel to West Berliners.

16. There were many differences in _____ between the Soviet Union and the West.

17. Germany was a(n) _____ in World War II.

18. Many communists were arrested during the _____.

19. In the _____, United States forces were sent to protect South Korea.

20. A key element of the Cold War was _____.

Notes for Home: Your child learned the vocabulary words from Chapter 9.
Home Activity: Ask your child to summarize what he or she learned in Chapter 9 using these words.

Name _____ Date _____

Vocabulary Preview

Directions: Match each vocabulary word to its meaning. Write the number of the word on the blank next to its meaning.

1. civil rights

2. passive resistance

3. space race

4. guerilla warfare

5. arms control

6. Vietnam Conflict

7. National Organization for Women

8. United Farm Workers of America

9. Americans with Disabilities Act

10. Equal Employment Opportunity Commission

11. Environmental Protection Agency

12. Earth Day

13. Persian Gulf War

14. Internet

_____ law that makes it illegal for businesses to refuse to hire a qualified person just because that person has a disability

_____ worldwide network of computers

_____ conflict in which United States forces fought alongside the South Vietnamese against the North Vietnamese

_____ conflict in which the United States led an alliance to force Iraq out of Kuwait

_____ rights that are guaranteed to all citizens by the Constitution

_____ organization that works to gain rights for migrant workers

_____ holiday designed to make people aware of ways they could help the environment

_____ deal to limit the production of weapons

_____ organization that works toward equal opportunities for women

_____ race to explore outer space

_____ commission that enforces civil rights laws that have to do with the workplace

_____ to oppose something without using violence

_____ agency created to enforce environmental laws

_____ war tactics that include surprise, random attacks

© Scott Foresman / Growth of a Nation

Notes for Home: Your child learned the vocabulary words from Chapter 10.
Home Activity: Help your child write sentences using these words.

Lesson 1: African Americans and Civil Rights

Directions: Complete the time line with information from this lesson. You may use your textbook.

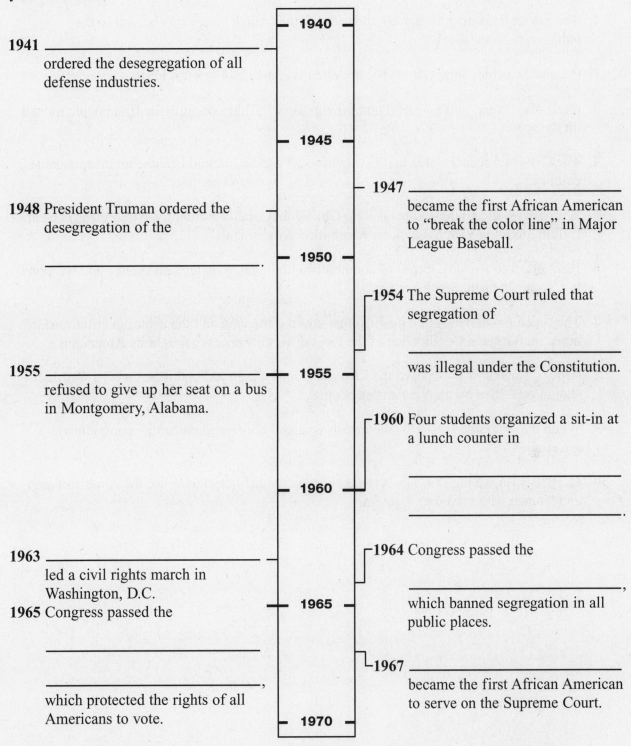

1941 _____ ordered the desegregation of all defense industries.

1948 President Truman ordered the desegregation of the

_____ .

1955 _____ refused to give up her seat on a bus in Montgomery, Alabama.

1963 _____ led a civil rights march in Washington, D.C.

1965 Congress passed the

_____

_____ ,

which protected the rights of all Americans to vote.

1940

1945

1947 _____ became the first African American to "break the color line" in Major League Baseball.

1950

1954 The Supreme Court ruled that segregation of

_____

was illegal under the Constitution.

1955

1960 Four students organized a sit-in at a lunch counter in

_____

_____ .

1960

1964 Congress passed the

_____ ,

which banned segregation in all public places.

1965

1967 _____ became the first African American to serve on the Supreme Court.

1970

Notes for Home: Your child learned about African Americans' efforts to gain civil rights in the 1950s and 1960s.
Home Activity: Discuss the concept of passive resistance with your child. Ask your child whether he or she thinks this was an effective strategy in the civil rights movement.

© Scott Foresman / Growth of a Nation

Lesson 2: The Cold War Continues

Directions: Using information from this lesson, circle the term in parentheses that best completes each sentence.

1. The Soviet launching of *Sputnik* showed that the United States was behind in the (space race, arms race).

2. (Michael Collins, John Glenn) became the first American to orbit Earth.

3. (Neil Armstrong, Yuri Gagarin) and Edwin "Buzz" Aldrin became the first people to walk on the moon.

4. The Geneva Accords stated that (Switzerland, Vietnam) should become an independent country.

5. With Soviet and Chinese support, (Ho Chi Minh, General William Westmoreland) began fighting to unite Vietnam under a communist government.

6. In an effort to stop the spread of communism, the United States sent money and weapons to (North Vietnam, South Vietnam).

7. The (open grasslands, thick jungles) that covered the land and the use of guerilla warfare made the Vietnam Conflict one of the most difficult wars ever fought by Americans.

8. (Doves, Hawks) who opposed the Vietnam Conflict believed that it was a civil war that should be settled by the Vietnamese people.

9. When the war ended in 1975, Vietnam was united under a (democratic, communist) government.

10. In 1980, (Maya Ying Lin, Jan Scruggs) designed a memorial to honor the American men and women who served in Vietnam.

© Scott Foresman / Growth of a Nation

Notes for Home: Your child learned about continuing Cold War tensions in the 1960s and 1970s.
Home Activity: Help your child write a letter to a newspaper editor as either a hawk or a dove during the Vietnam Conflict.

Name _____ Date _____

Lesson Review

Use with Pages 438–444.

Lesson 3: Years of Change

Directions: For each item below, describe how Americans worked for change. You
may use your textbook.

1. Women _____

   _____

   _____

2. Migrant Workers _____

   _____

   _____

   _____

3. Americans with Disabilities _____

   _____

   _____

   _____

   _____

4. The Environment _____

   _____

   _____

   _____

   _____

Directions: Describe different ways that people can work to protect the environment.
Use a separate sheet of paper if you need more space.

   _____

   _____

   _____

   _____

Notes for Home: Your child learned how Americans worked toward equal rights and gained interest in
protecting the environment.
Home Activity: Help your child use library or Internet resources to learn more about an environmental
issue of interest.

Lesson 4: Changing World, Changing Roles

Directions: Complete the chart with information from this lesson.

Who are they?	How did they help bring about change?
Richard Nixon	
Jimmy Carter	
Ronald Reagan	
Mikhail Gorbachev	
George Bush	
Condoleezza Rice	
Colin Powell	
Bill Clinton	
Madeleine Albright	
George W. Bush	

 Notes for Home: Your child learned about events that brought the Cold War to an end and put the United States on a new course for the future.
Home Activity: Talk with your child about changes that have taken place since the end of the Cold War.

© Scott Foresman / Growth of a Nation

Understand Map Projections

Directions: A map projection is a way of showing the round Earth on a flat surface.
All map projections have errors in size, shape, distance, or direction.

Map A

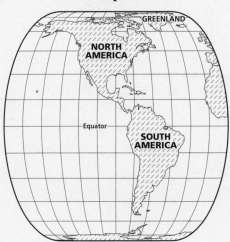

Map B

1. Which map uses the Mercator projection? How can you tell?

_____

_____

2. Which map uses an equal-area projection? How can you tell?

_____

_____

3. Describe the differences in the shape of North America on the two maps.

_____

_____

4. Which map would you use to compare the actual size of Greenland to North America?
Explain.

_____

_____

_____

Notes for Home: Your child learned about map projections and their distortions.
Home Activity: Study several maps in an atlas with your child. Ask your child to identify the type of map
projection and the distortions of each map.

Vocabulary Review

Directions: Draw a line from the vocabulary word to its meaning.

Column I	Column II
1. civil rights	**a.** race to explore outer space
2. passive resistance	**b.** deal to limit the production of weapons
3. space race	**c.** war tactics that include surprise and random attacks
4. guerilla warfare	**d.** rights that are guaranteed to all citizens by the Constitution
5. arms control	**e.** to oppose something without using violence

Directions: Use each of the vocabulary words in a sentence. You may use a separate sheet of paper if you need more space.

6. Vietnam Conflict _____

_____

7. National Organization for Women _____

_____

8. United Farm Workers of America _____

_____

9. Americans with Disabilities Act _____

_____

10. Equal Employment Opportunity Commission _____

_____

11. Earth Day _____

12. Environmental Protection Agency _____

_____

13. Persian Gulf War _____

_____

14. Internet _____

Notes for Home: Your child learned the vocabulary words from Chapter 10.
Home Activity: Ask your child to use these words to describe the changing United States in the late 1900s.

© Scott Foresman / Growth of a Nation

Name _____ Date _____

Use with Page 288.

^{UNIT} 5 Project **Then and Now**

Bring the past to life in a documentary. Form a group and plan a documentary about historic events, advances in technology, and changes in everyday life that occurred during a decade from the 1900s.

1. We chose the decade 19_____–19_____.

2. The (✔) shows which topics we researched:

   ___ historic events   ___ technological   ___ transportation   ___ entertainment
   advances

   ___ clothing   ___ home life   ___ education   ___ occupations

   ___ other: _____

3. The following people from the decade will speak for the documentary:

Name: _____ Role: _____

Name: _____ Role: _____

Name: _____ Role: _____

Name: _____ Role: _____

4. Questions and answers about living in the 19_____s:

_____

_____

_____

_____

✔ Checklist for Students

_____ The group chose a decade from the 1900s.

_____ The group researched topics about living in the 19_____s.

_____ Students assigned roles to each other for the documentary.

_____ The group wrote questions and answers about the decade.

_____ The group presented its documentary to the class.

Notes for Home: Your child participated in a group presentation on a decade from the 1900s.
Home Activity: Discuss with your child your favorite decade of the twentieth century. Describe the clothing, home life, transportation, and important events of this time period.

Summarize

Directions: Summarizing means telling the main idea of a paragraph, section, or story. Read the passage below. Then fill in the circle next to the correct answer for each question that follows.

The United States is a country made up of fifty unique states and a diverse population. One of the reasons that the United States is so diverse is that immigrants have come here from all over the world. About 1,000 years ago, Europeans began traveling to North America as explorers. Portugal was the first nation to send explorers. Next, Spain sent people such as Christopher Columbus and Juan Ponce de León. The English sent John Cabot and Henry Hudson to explore the coast of North America. French explorers such as Jacques Cartier and Samuel de Champlain eventually arrived, landing in what is now Canada. Over the course of our nation's history, many people also arrived from Africa, Asia, and European nations including Ireland, Italy, Poland, and Germany. Today the largest immigrant populations are from Asia and Latin America. In all, people from about 200 different countries live in the United States.

---

1. Which sentence best summarizes why the United States is so diverse?

   Ⓐ There were always many European explorers.

   Ⓑ About 1,000 years ago, Portugal became the first nation to send explorers.

   Ⓒ Immigrants have come to the United States from all over the world.

   Ⓓ The United States is a country made up of fifty unique states.

2. According to this paragraph, from which continent did some of the earliest explorers come to North America?

   Ⓐ Africa

   Ⓑ Australia

   Ⓒ Latin America

   Ⓓ Europe

3. Which sentence best summarizes what the population of the United States is like today?

   Ⓐ People from about 200 different countries live in the United States.

   Ⓑ The United States is a country made up of fifty unique states.

   Ⓒ Many immigrants have come from Europe.

   Ⓓ European explorers established colonies that are now states.

© Scott Foresman / Growth of a Nation

Notes for Home: Your child learned to summarize and identify important details from a passage.
Home Activity: Read a newspaper article with your child. Together, summarize the main idea and identify important details.

Vocabulary Preview

Directions: These are the vocabulary terms for Chapter 11. Circle the term that best matches the definition or description below it.

1. **citizen   producer**

   a member of a country

2. **import   export**

   a good that is sold to other countries

3. **interdependence   democracy**

   a government in which all people have a say in how the government is run

4. **ideals   demand**

   important beliefs

5. **Legislative Branch   electoral college**

   the special system of voting in the United States

6. **electoral college   ethnic group**

   a group of people who share the same customs and language

7. **Legislative Branch   Executive Branch**

   part of the government that makes the laws

8. **Judicial Branch   Legislative Branch**

   part of the government that interprets the laws

9. **region   Sunbelt**

   a large area that has common features that set it apart from other areas

10. **democracy   interdependence**

    situation in which one country's economy can affect the economics of other countries

Vocabulary Preview (continued)

11. supply   demand

the amount of a product that is available

12. opportunity cost   ideals

the value of what must be given up in order to produce a certain good

13. Executive Branch   Judicial Branch

part of the government that makes sure laws are carried out

14. globalization   popular sovereignty

a government in which the people rule

15. demand   supply

the amount of a product that people are willing to buy

16. producer   citizen

person who makes goods

17. ethnic group   Sunbelt

the Southeast and Southwest regions of the United States

18. interdependence   North American Free Trade Agreement

an agreement that allows the United States, Canada, and Mexico to import from and export to each other without having to pay taxes or fees

19. opportunity cost   globalization

the development of a world economic system

20. import   export

a good that one country buys from another country

© Scott Foresman / Growth of a Nation

Notes for Home: Your child previewed the vocabulary terms for Chapter 11.
Home Activity: With your child, write each vocabulary term on an index card and each definition on a separate card. Shuffle the cards and turn them all facedown. Then have your child turn cards over one at a time to match each term with its definition. Be sure to turn the unmatched cards facedown again.

Lesson 1: The Fifty States

Directions: Draw a line from the state in Column I to its region in Column II.

Column I	Column II
1. California	**a.** Northeast
2. Michigan	**b.** Southeast
3. Texas	**c.** Midwest
4. New York	**d.** Southwest
5. Florida	**e.** West

Directions: Complete the following sentences with information from your textbook.

6. The population of the _____ began to increase after World War II.

7. The population of many older cities in the Northeast and _____ has declined.

8. The motto *E Pluribus Unum,* found on the Great Seal of the United States, means

   _____ .

9. Today most immigrants come to the United States from Latin America and

   _____ .

10. When writer _____ moved to New York City from Puerto Rico, she learned to speak and write in English.

Notes for Home: Your child learned about the states and regions of the United States.
Home Activity: With your child, locate your own state on a map. Then discuss the geography and the climate of the region in which you live.

Name _____ Date _____

Compare Population Density Maps

Directions: A population density map is a type of distribution map that shows how population is spread out over an area. Look at the maps below. Then answer the questions that follow.

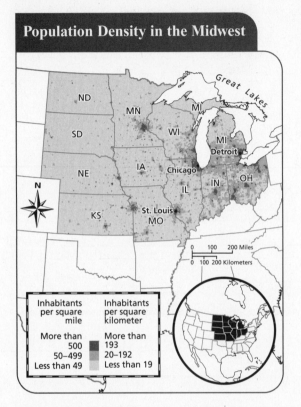

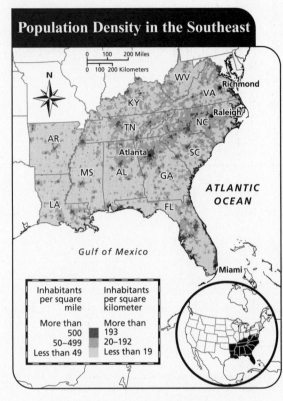

1. Based on the maps, is the population more evenly distributed in the Southeast or the Midwest? Explain.

   _____

   _____

   _____

   _____

2. Which state is more densely populated, North Carolina or North Dakota?

   _____

3. What generalization can you make about the population density near the major cities shown on the maps?

   _____

Notes for Home: Your child learned to compare population density maps.
Home Activity: Work with your child to find out which areas of your state are most densely populated. You might consult the U.S. Census Bureau Web site or an almanac. Discuss why these areas might be more densely populated than other areas.

© Scott Foresman / Growth of a Nation

Lesson 2: Government of the People

Directions: Finish the partially completed chart below with information about the three branches of the United States government.

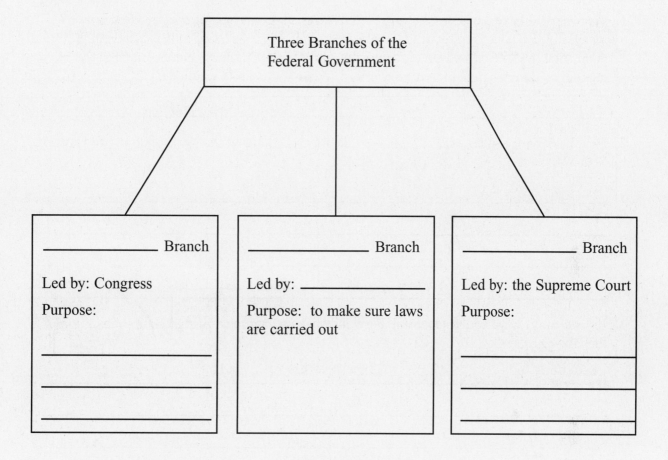

Three Branches of the
Federal Government

_____ Branch

Led by: Congress

Purpose:

_____

_____

_____

_____ Branch

Led by: _____

Purpose: to make sure laws are carried out

_____ Branch

Led by: the Supreme Court

Purpose:

_____

_____

_____

Directions: Answer the questions on the lines provided.

1. What do we mean when we say that the United States is a democracy?

_____

_____

2. Why do we use the electoral college for national elections?

_____

_____

Notes for Home: Your child learned about the United States government.
Home Activity: Talk about what living in a democracy means to you. Then ask your child to explain what he or she believes is good about the United States government. Encourage him or her to point to specific examples.

Name _____ Date _____

Lesson 3: Economy and Trade

Directions: Respond to the following questions on the lines provided. You may use
your textbook.

1. Suppose you have a business selling pencils with a special type of eraser. There aren't
   many of these pencils around, so people are willing to pay a lot of money for them. You set
   your price high. Eventually, a big company starts producing these pencils in large
   quantities. You now must lower your prices. What is this an example of?

   _____

2. How have both computers and improved health care changed the job market in the United
   States?

   _____

   _____

   _____

3. In what ways have computer technology and space technology changed communication in
   the United States?

   _____

   _____

   _____

4. Generally, how do Americans today feel about international trade?

   _____

   _____

5. What is an effect of globalization on the world?

   _____

   _____

© Scott Foresman / Growth of a Nation

Notes for Home: Your child learned about how technology and changing attitudes toward international
trade have affected life in the United States and throughout the world.
Home Activity: With your child, list ways in which technology is part of your lives at home, school, and
work. Then talk about ways in which increased international trade affects your lives. Point out products in
your household that come from other countries.

Internet Research

Directions: Answer the following questions on the lines provided.

1. What is one advantage of doing research on the Internet?

   _____

   _____

2. What is one disadvantage of doing research on the Internet?

   _____

   _____

3. Which types of Web sites offer the most reliable information?

   _____

   _____

4. When using a search engine, what is the effect of putting a phrase in quotes?

   _____

Directions: Suppose your friend wants to research satellites and other examples of space technology in our everyday lives. In the space below, describe the steps your friend might take to find this information on the Internet.

_____

_____

_____

_____

_____

_____

_____

_____

Notes for Home: Your child learned about doing research on the Internet.
Home Activity: Work with your child on your home or local library computer to research a topic of your child's choice.

© Scott Foresman / Growth of a Nation

Vocabulary Review

Directions: Write a definition of each vocabulary term on the lines provided. Use a separate sheet of paper if necessary. You may use your glossary.

1. region _____

   _____

2. Sunbelt _____

   _____

3. ideals _____

   _____

4. ethnic group _____

   _____

5. democracy _____

   _____

6. popular sovereignty _____

   _____

7. citizen _____

   _____

8. electoral college _____

   _____

9. Legislative Branch _____

   _____

10. Executive Branch _____

    _____

Vocabulary Review (continued)

11. Judicial Branch _____

_____

12. supply _____

_____

13. demand _____

_____

14. producer _____

_____

15. opportunity cost _____

_____

16. export _____

_____

17. import _____

_____

18. North American Free Trade Agreement _____

_____

_____

19. globalization _____

_____

20. interdependence _____

_____

 Notes for Home: Your child learned the vocabulary terms from Chapter 11.
Home Activity: Discuss with your child how each term relates to the fifty states, the United States government, or the economy of the United States.

Vocabulary Preview

Directions: These are the vocabulary terms from Chapter 12. Match the underlined term in each sentence with its example or definition below. Write the term on the line provided. You may use your glossary.

- In the terrorist attack on September 11, 2001, more than 3,000 people from more than 90 different countries were killed.

- The agreement that ended the Persian Gulf War included a promise that Iraq would destroy all weapons of mass destruction.

- Scientists are investigating the long-term effects of the increase of carbon dioxide in our atmosphere.

- Some scientists believe that an increase in carbon dioxide is leading to global warming.

- At some universities, scientists are working to build machines with artificial intelligence.

_____ **1.** the mass of gases that surround a planet

_____ **2.** technology that gives a machine the ability to learn and to imitate human thought

_____ **3.** a person who uses violence and fear to try to achieve goals

_____ **4.** a slow warming of Earth's climate

_____ **5.** nuclear weapons and weapons that spread poison chemicals or deadly diseases

Notes for Home: Your child previewed the vocabulary terms from Chapter 12.
Home Activity: Ask your child what he or she has heard about these terms. Talk about how the terms represent issues that concern people right now.

Lesson 1: New Dangers

Directions: Tell how each person or group relates to the events of September 11, 2001, or the American response to these events.

1. Rudolph Giuliani _____

_____

_____

2. George W. Bush and Condoleezza Rice _____

_____

_____

_____

3. al Qaeda and Osama bin Laden _____

_____

_____

_____

Directions: Respond to the following questions on the lines provided.

4. Why did the United States go to war in Afghanistan?

_____

_____

_____

_____

5. Why did some people believe war against Iraq was necessary? Why did some people believe war was unnecessary?

_____

_____

_____

_____

Notes for Home: Your child learned about the different ways in which Americans responded to the terrorist attacks of September 11, 2001.
Home Activity: Talk to your child about the continued effects of the events of September 11, 2001, on life in the United States. Ask how he or she feels about America's response to these attacks.

© Scott Foresman / Growth of a Nation

Lesson 2: Looking Ahead

Directions: Complete the chart with information from this lesson. For each category, tell how people are working toward change. You may use your textbook.

Global Warming	
Disease	
Brain Damage	
Artificial Intelligence	
Space Technology	

© Scott Foresman / Growth of a Nation

Notes for Home: Your child learned how people are working to develop new technologies and find solutions to global challenges.
Home Activity: Ask your child to identify a global challenge of the twenty-first century. Help your child use library or Internet resources to learn about the different ways people are working toward a solution to the problem.

Make Generalizations

Directions: A generalization is a broad statement or idea about a subject. Read the following passage and answer the questions that follow on the lines provided.

> Life has changed a great deal in the United States over the past 100 years. Inventions have made life more comfortable and convenient, but they have also made life more complicated. For example, cars, jet airplanes, and other modern forms of transportation have become part of everyday life. Electricity, running water, and heat have become available to most people. Changes such as these have impacted society in positive ways. There are responsibilities that go along with these changes, however. For example, the burning of gasoline and coal produces gases that can be harmful to the atmosphere. People must work to try to find new sources of energy and improve the ones already available to us so we do not do more harm to our environment.

1. What is the main idea of this paragraph?

   _____

   _____

2. What is one statement in the paragraph that is a generalization?

   _____

   _____

3. What generalization can you make based on the passage?

   _____

   _____

4. Review Lesson 2 of Chapter 12. Make one generalization about a topic covered in the lesson, such as protecting the environment, solving global problems, or looking ahead to challenges of the future.

   _____

   _____

Notes for Home: Your child learned how to make generalizations.
Home Activity: With your child, practice making both true and false generalizations about events in your daily lives. Discuss what types of mistakes lead to false generalizations.

Vocabulary Review

Directions: Draw a line from each term to its meaning. You may use your glossary.

1. weapons of mass destruction

2. terrorist

3. atmosphere

4. global warming

5. artificial intelligence

a. the mass of gases that surround a planet

b. the ability of machines to learn and imitate human thought

c. slow warming of the global climate

d. person who uses violence and fear to try to achieve goals

e. nuclear weapons and weapons that spread poison chemicals or deadly diseases

Directions: Use each of the vocabulary terms from Chapter 12 in a sentence. Write your sentences on the lines provided.

_____

_____

_____

_____

_____

_____

_____

_____

_____

_____

_____

_____

Notes for Home: Your child learned the vocabulary terms from Chapter 12.
Home Activity: Ask your child to summarize what he or she learned in Chapter 12 using these terms.

Discovery
CHANNEL
SCHOOL

Use with Page 528.

UNIT 6 Project Explore a Business

In a group, plan and make a presentation about a product or a business.

1. The product or business we chose is _____.

2. Below is some information about the product or business. The (✔) shows the specific areas we plan to cover in our presentation:

____ Value and cost: _____

_____

____ History: _____

_____

_____

____ Its successes: _____

_____

_____

____ How it helps the economy: _____

_____

_____

3. Our advertisement on a poster or banner will show: _____

_____

✔ Checklist for Students

____ We chose and researched a product or business.

____ We wrote a script for a presentation about the product.

____ We made an advertisement on a poster or banner.

____ We presented our product or business to the class.

Notes for Home: Your child chose and researched a product or business and helped present it to his or her class.
Home Activity: Have a discussion with your child about products and businesses that are important to your local economy.

NOTES

NOTES

NOTES

NOTES

NOTES

NOTES

NOTES

NOTES

NOTES

NOTES

NOTES